BOOKS BY DAVID R. EYLER

Resumes That Mean Business

More Than Friends, Less Than Lovers: Managing Sexual Attraction in the Workplace (written with Andrea Baridon)

Sexual Harassment Awareness Training (written with Andrea Baridon)

Starting and Operating a Home-Based Business

The Executive Moonlighter: Building Your Next Career Without Leaving Your Present Job

The Home Business Bible

Working Together: The New Rules and Realities for Managing Men and Women at Work (written with Andrea Baridon)

JOB INTERVIEWS

THAT MEAN

BUSINESS

JOB INTERVIEWS

RANDOM HOUSE

New York

THAT MEAN
BUSINESS

THIRD EDITION

DAVID R. EYLER

Typeset and printed in the United States of America.
Typeset by Allentown Digital Services, an RR Donnelly & Sons Company

Library of Congress Catalog Card Number: 99-70176

Third Edition
0 9 8 7 6 5 4 3 2 1
March 1999

ISBN 0-375-70470-1

New York   Toronto   London   Sydney   Auckland

To the lesser bosses who would have
fired us—and the lesser men and women
who would have quit!

CONTENTS

PREFACE

Job Interviews That Mean Business is a practical guide to prepare you for your job interview. It covers the employment cycle from finding a job and securing an interview through following up and ultimately negotiating your terms of employment. The objective is to increase your chances of doing each of these things successfully. By reading this book you gain the kind of understanding and confidence that only comes from knowing the hiring process and mastering the techniques that impress interviewers.

It follows the sequence of the actual hiring cycle, giving you advice on:

- how to find a job;
- how to get an interview;
- how to prepare for the interview;
- how to arrive and present yourself for the interview;
- what to say and not say during the interview;
- what to do and not do during the interview;
- how to interpret the messages sent by the interviewer;
- how to link the entire interview cycle into a smooth and complete presentation of your assets;
- how to avoid surprises—and deal with the ones that come anyway;
- what kinds of questions to expect from your interviewer;

- what to ask your interviewer;
- how to enhance the impact of your interview by networking;
- how to follow up effectively; and
- how to negotiate salary and terms of employment.

Included is a chapter on technology and the interview that contains sections on videotaped interviews, satellite and computer-supported interviewing, background checking, psychological testing, handwriting analysis, and other means employers use to evaluate your personality, character, honesty, and aptitudes. Another chapter discusses how the Internet can help you prepare for a successful interview. Legal matters such as discrimination and privacy are covered for you, with an emphasis on practical rather than adversarial advice. A chapter addresses the role sexual attraction might play at interview time and how to deal with it. While the primary emphasis is on mainstream candidates, a concluding chapter provides help for interviewees in the following categories:

- older workers;
- women returning to the job market;
- candidates interviewing after being fired;
- candidates new to this country, its culture, and its hiring procedures;
- candidates competing for a position beneath the status they previously held—that is, convincing others that you can accept less;
- early retirees seeking a second career; and
- students securing a first professional position.

The purpose of *Job Interviews That Mean Business* is to prepare you for the important first meeting with your new employer and colleagues. Your newfound knowledge will help you make the most of the opportunity. From the moment you express interest to your acceptance of the job offer, this book will help you take your next step up the career ladder.

David R. Eyler
eylerd@worldnet.att.net

Arlington, Virginia
September, 1998

INTRODUCTION

Preparing yourself for a winning job interview is an exercise in mobilizing your assets. You craft a practical image of who and what you are, and then refine it with a thorough knowledge of

- company needs;
- interviewer style and objectives; and
- self-control based on a meticulous understanding of what is going on.

You can have a more successful interview by studying the process, understanding the role you play as the hiring sequence unfolds, and preparing effectively. The purpose of this book is to inform, to give you the benefit of many examples and much comparison among candidates experiencing the various situations of the interview process. From it emerge rules and suggestions for the right and the wrong ways of playing your role, but in the end it is you, the candidate, who must decide just what combination of substance and methodology makes the best case for your particular talents. The judge who counts most is the interviewer, the human resources professional, line manager, or CEO who, after your interview, decides if you are the right person for the job.

Using This Book

This is a "how to do it" book, from which you will choose the parts that are the most important and useful to you in your particular situation. Still, most of the information will be helpful to all people. Read this section carefully; it will guide you to exactly what you need.

THE "HOW TO" INDEX

In the front of this book you will find a special index to

- the interview process overviews;
- case histories that illustrate interview situations and techniques,
- lists and tables containing helpful information; and
- chapter summary checklists.

The index is an immediate pointer to just the information you need to solve a specific problem. It refers you to practical advice that you will want to refer back to after reading the complete book.

THE INTERVIEW PROCESS

The first part of this book assists you in preparing for the interview itself. It shows you how to find the job and get the interview, prepare for it once it is imminent, and make arrangements for appearing on time and composed. You are shown how to conduct yourself during the interview session, the right way to follow through when the appointment ends, and finally, how to negotiate terms and accept the position. Chapters 1 through 5 take you through the complete interview process.

INTERVIEW PROCESS OVERVIEWS

You can get lost in the complexities of the interview cycle if you don't keep your focus on the task before you. Each section of Part One, "The Interview Process," starts with an overview of the whole hiring cycle and a capsule view of what you should be concentrating on then—and why. With this graphic orientation to where you have been and what comes next, you can identify your strengths and bring them to bear on the task to carry you successfully to the next step.

CASE HISTORIES OF INTERVIEW SITUATIONS AND TECHNIQUES

Advice becomes practical as you relive instances where other job seekers have actually experienced the problems and applied the recommended solutions. Here each case is analyzed to show you the general strategy behind it, with ten key points noted about the situation and the techniques used to deal with it successfully.

LISTS AND TABLES

Throughout the book there are bulleted lists and tabular summaries of the information you really need to know about a topic. The "How to" index lists them by their functional titles.

CHAPTER SUMMARY CHECKLISTS

At the end of each chapter is a bulleted checklist recapping the major points of the chapter. Review the checklists to help remember important information and to see the purposeful actions you should take.

MORE INTERVIEWING STRATEGIES

TECHNOLOGY AND THE INTERVIEW

Job interviewing is still basically a matter of preparing yourself with company information and a comfortably rehearsed statement of your own assets. But technology is beginning to play a role in the process. While that role is still a limited one, Chapter 6, "Technology and the Interview," prepares you for the possibility that you will encounter such things as videotaped resumes, satellite conferences, and computerized interviews. It also tells you the latest techniques for dealing with preemployment testing, ranging from the psychological (personality and ability) to the physiological (drug and HIV), and from the lie detector (polygraph) to handwriting analysis (graphology).

USING THE INTERNET

The latest thing to impact job search, including the interview, is the Internet. Candidates can now use their personal computers to do everything from research job vacancies and potential employers to price homes in their new communities. The Internet also adds a new commandment to the job interviewer's bible: Thou shalt be familiar with thy company's web page.

INTERVIEWING AND THE LAW

It is unlikely that you will find it necessary to exercise your legal rights in the course of your job interview, but Chapter 8, "Interviewing and the Law," makes you aware of your basic rights—just in case you do. You are informed of the roles of government agencies and private groups concerned with fairness in the preemployment process.

SEX AND THE INTERVIEW

Sexual attraction is a subtle factor that might intrude on your interview, with or without conscious intent by you or the interviewer. Chapter 9, "Sex and the Interview," prepares you to react realistically and in your own self-interest instead of allowing it to become an unduly awkward moment that could destroy your chances of landing the job. With women and men in both the interviewer and candidate seats these days, sexual attraction is a possibility you need to be prepared to handle.

SPECIAL SITUATIONS

If you are not following a traditional career path to your next interview, read Chapter 10, "Special Situations." There is helpful advice for everyone in the following predicaments:

- people interviewing for less prestigious positions than they used to have;
- students seeking their first professional positions or part-time employment leading to them;
- early retirees from the military or other careers looking for new jobs;
- individuals interested in nontraditional working arrangements that offer greater flexibility; and
- new citizens and foreign workers uncertain about communicating their skills in the American workplace.

JOB SEARCH CORRESPONDENCE

It isn't wise to apply for a job using a book (or computer program) of "enter your name here" form letters. On the other hand, samples of well-crafted letters that address various situations can be useful models to emulate. Chapter 11, "Writing the Letters," provides a selection of good job candidate letters from which to draw ideas and build effective correspondence of your own. The examples are followed by comments that stress what to include and what to avoid in your job search correspondence.

So from the first steps of researching the company through the exacting task of fielding the difficult questions, *Job Interviews That Mean Business* is your personal tutor, showing you how to do things right. Following its guidance you avoid surprises, make the all-important connections between the separate events of the hiring cycle, recover graciously from setbacks, make key decisions correctly, and exit the interview process with the position you want.

"HOW TO" INDEX

Interview Process Overviews

Flip through Figures 1 through 8 to get an instant overview (or timely review) of the interview process. The annotated outlines appear on the following pages:

Case Histories Illustrating Techniques

Here is a ready reference for special topics that will assist you at various times in the interview process. The content is self-evident by the title of the particular case history; you can select the one needed for your situation of the moment. The case histories (each accompanied by an analysis) will be found on these pages:

Lists and Tables

The topics listed below are presentations of information on various subjects as indicated. These topics are found on the following pages:

Chapter Summary Checklists

Each chapter ends with a summary of the major points it contains. You might benefit by scanning these to refresh your memory or guide your use of the book. Here are the chapter summaries and the pages where you can find them:

Job Search Correspondence

PART

I

THE INTERVIEW PROCESS

1

GETTING THE INTERVIEW

You have to make three things happen before an interview is possible:

1. find the job;
2. apply for it; and
3. work your application to the top of the stack.

To be really effective, you need to understand the dynamics of the preliminary selection process—the things that go on before the first candidate is selected for an interview. This is necessary so you can judge when to make things happen, when to leave well enough alone, and precisely what to do when it is time to act. You must verify the true availability of the position and determine whether you stand a chance of being seriously considered—is it worth your time and effort? One way to get behind the scenes in a job search and generally improve your chances of turning an interview into a job is by networking to strengthen your candidacy. Finally, there are techniques that can improve your odds of getting that interview. This chapter addresses all of these tricks of the trade and more in these specific topics:

- finding the job;
- preliminary selection process;
- finding out if the job is really available;
- sensing when to take the initiative;
- networking your way to an interview;

- improving your odds of getting an interview; and
- why your interview is important to the employer.

Before you begin, look at the outline of the entire interview process in Figure 1 and orient yourself to what you are going to accomplish at the "Getting the Interview" stage. This is the stage where you find the job, determine how to apply for the job, and plan to make the most of the personal assets you will be presenting to your interviewer. At this point you lay the groundwork for everything that follows. What you learn becomes the basis for your personal preparations, getting ready to appear for the interview, what you do during the interview, the way you end your visit, appraising how you did, conducting your follow-up activities, and finally, negotiating the terms of accepting the position.

With that in mind, take a moment to review the stream of activity summarized in Figure 1 before going on to the particulars of "Getting the Interview."

Finding the Job

Unless you are in the unusual position of being actively courted by employers, you have to take personal initiatives to locate a job. Here are the options open to most people:

- reading newspapers and professional publications;
- listening for word-of-mouth leads;
- looking at bulletin boards;
- distributing letters and resumes;
- contacting executive recruiters to market you;
- making cold calls;
- self-advertising;
- using an outplacement firm;
- using an "expanded resume service"; and
- using the Internet.

NEWSPAPERS AND PROFESSIONAL PUBLICATIONS

Go to the library and look through every current and recent publication that would logically advertise for people with your qualifications. Make notes on everything

GETTING THE INTERVIEW
- Finding a job
- Applying
- Networking
- Getting invited

You become aware of the vacant position, identify the person who makes the hiring decision, and determine the procedures of the application process. Next you prepare and submit the best possible combination of your cover letter, resume, and the application form. You network widely and determine whom you know who might tell you behind-the-scenes details about the job, company, and people involved—or put in a favorable word on your behalf. Finally, you make the right telephone calls, exert what influence you have, position yourself to be available, and generally do what you can to get invited for an interview.

PREPARING FOR THE INTERVIEW
- Researching the company
- Preparing personally
- Anticipating questions

APPEARING FOR THE INTERVIEW
- Reconnaissance
- Personal readiness
- Timing

DURING THE INTERVIEW
- Names and personalities
- Style and substance
- Satisfying agendas

LEAVING THE INTERVIEW
- Reading your audience
- Positive expectations
- Last impression

EVALUATING YOUR INTERVIEW
- Substantive match
- Personal chemistry
- Judging your chances

FOLLOWING UP AFTER YOUR INTERVIEW
- Thank you's
- Additional information
- More networking

CONCLUDING THE INTERVIEW PROCESS
- The offer
- Negotiating
- Accepting

Figure 1. Getting the Interview

that interests you or looks as though it might be close enough to get you noticed for something more appropriate. Note the names and addresses of points of contact— even if the job isn't what you are looking for at the moment. Set priorities and concentrate on current openings first. Get the big picture of which companies are hiring, and use that knowledge in your interview preparation. This kind of information helps you tap the "hidden" job market—positions that are not currently advertised but that are ready to be filled. Executive recruiters rely heavily on such finds as they market promising candidates. Success often comes for them (and for you) when the right resume is presented at the right time—which is *not* necessarily limited to when everyone else is responding to an advertised vacancy.

BULLETIN BOARDS

Depending on your specialty, you can sometimes walk through buildings housing companies in your field and find jobs posted. You can also take advantage of in-house postings by having your friends look where they work. Government agencies and public employers have bulletin boards full of advertised positions—many require that you already be in the civil service system, but look and inquire. Doing so can generate other leads. Office buildings have lobby bulletin boards posted with index cards seeking everything from clerical help to managers—sometimes to fill short-term, grant-generated positions that can lead to a permanent job.

Don't overlook these obvious sources. Dress for business, have your briefcase full of resumes, and walk right in if the posted vacancy lends itself to such an approach. If you don't see the bulletin board, ask where it is located. If the lobby security desk is an obstacle, select a company name from the directory and indicate that you are there to check on a position with that firm. When you get to the receptionist, ask to see their job vacancy announcements. The worst case is that they have none. You are inside now; visit as many offices as possible, leave resumes, make contacts for the future, and have ad hoc interviews as they present themselves.

ELECTRONIC ONLINE SERVICES

Computer online services are the electronic equivalent of posting jobs and broadcasting resumes. Free services are sponsored by specialized professional groups— inquire with organizations and publications that represent your field. Commercial services are also available; with these you pay a fee to post your resume and examine job listings. *Resumes That Mean Business, Third Edition* (Random House, 1999) devotes a chapter to electronic resumes and services.

WORD OF MOUTH

Networking is one of your richest sources of current vacancy information. Talk to people who work where you would like to become employed. Let them know that you are interested in hearing about opportunities for which you might apply. Give them an informal sketch of your professional background if they are not already aware of it and ask them to serve as a listening post for you—give them a resume. As a rule, people are complimented and welcome the chance to help.

LETTERS AND RESUMES

Go to the library and use business directories for researching companies. If you need help, examine the *Directory of Directories* or talk with the librarian about where to begin your search. Mail the letter and resume on a speculative basis, noting your interest in the company. Show you know what the company does, and indicate how you could play a useful role in its operation. In *Resumes That Mean Business,* I describe "market letters" and "notices of availability" that can be used effectively to canvass for positions. Examine that technique and decide whether it might be more effective than resumes and cover letters in your particular situation.

EXECUTIVE RECRUITERS

If you have a highly marketable skill, take advantage of an executive recruiter to comb the marketplace for you. The first test of a reputable recruiter is that you pay the recruiter nothing—the company that hires you pays the fee. You can bet that the recruiter will not waste valuable time on you unless there is a good chance of collecting that fee. A recruiter's interest is one of the most honest appraisals of your market value—assuming he or she isn't disinterested merely because you fall outside his or her narrow recruiting specialty. Should you encounter indifference, ask if it is because you are outside his or her field of interest, and seek a referral. Case History 1 illustrates the technique.

Don't confuse executive recruiters with placement firms who charge to find you a job—that is an entirely different business. Check the executive recruiter directories and contact a few of the firms that operate in your specialty. (See sample letter on page 222.) Do not list yourself with every firm. Recruiters will inevitably bump into each other marketing you and could decide further effort on their part isn't worthwhile. First, pick one good recruiter, give him or her an exclusive for a reasonable period of time, and see what he or she can do. Ask whether you will be actively marketed or become part of a database for vacancies as they occur.

Case History 1—Situation

EXECUTIVE RECRUITER INTEREST TEST

Background

Nancy Johnston is in her third year as a systems analyst with a defense contractor. ❶ She is receptive to relocating nationally but reluctant to send her resume all over the industry without assurance of interest and confidentiality. She decides that if an executive recruiter will market her effectively, that is the best way to accomplish her move. However, she has heard recruiter promises before and wants to be sure she has a recruiter who will actively market her. ❷

Situation

❸ Nancy calls a recruiter who contacted her several times in the past seeking her advice on people who might be suitable candidates for positions he was filling. She knew that part of his strategy was to interest her in relocating, but ❹ she still feels comfortable with his way of doing business. ❺ He responds positively, and they talk that evening by telephone from her home so she can speak freely. That call is an exciting one, with the recruiter helping to target her interests and ❻ informing her about several opportunities he will explore right away. ❼ Within a few days, Nancy is having brief conferences with her recruiter every day or so—confirming something in her preparation that mattered to a particular employer, ❽ verifying the name of her supervisor so a prospective employer could make a professional inquiry, testing interest in certain kinds of jobs, and asking about the ❾ acceptability of relocating to a West Coast city within the month.

Conclusion

Nancy sees the activity of her recruiter grow from information-gathering to active presentation of her credentials in a few weeks' time. ❿ Her conversations turn to arranging telephone interviews, making appointments for face-to-face discussions with hiring officials in distant cities, and finally, negotiating an offer. She is not a passive file resume to her recruiter. This shows in specific activity and results.

Case History 1—Analysis

EXECUTIVE RECRUITER INTEREST TEST

General Strategy

Nancy knows the problem with sending her own resume and takes a more surgical approach to reaching prospective employers. She knows that a good recruiter could do the job, but needs evidence that the recruiter is convinced of her marketability. This evidence comes from a quick response to her statement of interest and almost immediate third-party interaction with employers showing actual interest from the field.

Specific Points

❶ Recruiters do what you cannot do for yourself—target your resume to the right people directly and discreetly.

❷ Your challenge is to find a recruiter who will do more than make you a routine "listing"—you want evidence that you will be *actively* marketed, or you might as well sign up with a national job bank.

❸ If you are in a high-demand field, you have already had contact with a recruiter or know of colleagues who have.

❹ Step one in deciding on a recruiter is finding comfort with his or her style.

❺ Agreeing on objectives and the realistic prospects for fulfilling them is essential to making progress together.

❻ Your first sign of valid recruiter interest is his or her questioning you about situations that he or she is actively working. If you are really marketable, this conversation takes place up front.

❼ Your confirmation that real activity is taking place is when you receive calls for more information and clarification from your recruiter.

❽ Actual contact arranged between principals means that you are being considered seriously as a result of the recruiter's efforts.

❾ Relocation inquiries come only from potential offers.

❿ Nancy's evidence of marketability and recruiter interest? Real activity.

If you find someone who will actively market you, you have arrived. When you are getting preferred treatment, there will be noticeable activity. You will get inquiries for more detailed information from the recruiter as he or she finds interest among the employers contacted. Telephone interviews will be scheduled. A good recruiter who is really interested in you will engage you in a very active process. Any status short of that with a recruiter is of limited value. The real action (and endorsement of your market value) is in being an actively marketed candidate.

COLD CALLS

If you are willing to take an active role on your own behalf, use the directories of your profession and call people who would have a potential interest in hiring you.

- Let them know that you are available.
- Tell them what your qualifications are.
- Ask if they have any vacancies.
- If they don't have any vacancies, inquire as to who might need your services now.

In effect, you become your own executive recruiter. As you will learn, it isn't especially easy or fun—a lot of people say no. However, persistent cold calling to the right kind of people uncovers jobs you would never find in a passive, traditional job search. It puts you into an active mode that few of your job-hunting competitors will have the initiative to match—most people are uncomfortable at the very thought of this approach. If you can do it, you will greatly increase your chances of finding a good job. Here are some rules to keep in mind.

Rules for Being Your Own Executive Recruiter

- Know what you want to do and why you are hunting for a job. (Have a positive, professional, and career-oriented reason ready if asked.)
- Begin with a simple script that can guide you until it becomes automatic: "Good morning, Ms. Jones, my name is Penny Moss. I am a commercial loan officer with four years of experience successfully developing new business with midmarket companies. I'm looking for a professional growth opportunity, and I thought you'd be interested in talking with me." Then let the other person speak, but be ready to react and keep the conversation going as interest develops.

- Engage your contact's interest by a compliment about his or her company (if you have the basis for a valid one from your research) and a brief, convincing line or two about what you can do for the company.

- Respond to signs of interest (What's your major? Have you ever...? How much are you making? [Stall this particular one by saying something like "I'm sure you could be competitive!," but recognize it as a "buy signal" and keep the conversation going.])

- Lock in the next step by setting up an interview, or at least another call. Never settle for "send me a resume" unless the request is linked to a more valid expression of interest, such as those just mentioned. Otherwise it's usually a brush-off and not worth your time and postage. Explain that you are only interested in current positions and are sensitive about circulating your resume without a specific job objective—then push for the particulars about what she or he has in mind. If nothing, forget it and make your next call.

- Gain "market knowledge"—find out what is going on in your industry, where the next opportunities are going to be in this contact's opinion.

- Identify another good lead somewhere else if she or he doesn't need you just now—don't be bashful about asking specific questions such as:

  - ✓ Whom do you know who could use someone with my preparation?

  - ✓ Who is expanding their operation and might be staffing?

  - ✓ Is there someone elsewhere in your company who might have an interest in someone like me?

  - ✓ May I say that you suggested I call?

If you need more detailed information on how an executive recruiter operates, refer to my book *The Executive Moonlighter* (John Wiley & Sons, 1989).

SELF-ADVERTISING

The "Positions Wanted" columns of the classified sections are small because job seekers read these pages more than employers do. While some people may find work by advertising their own talents, a more active approach will get more leads in a shorter time.

OUTPLACEMENT FIRMS

Outplacement firms are a passive sort of executive recruitment organization at which you are assisted in identifying your potential and finding a place to use it. The firms are less worried about having a highly marketable candidate because they get paid for helping candidates, not placing them. A good outplacement organization has helpful knowledge of the job market and can assist, but it is not a service to purchase on your own. If your company provides it, use it and hope for the best; some are very good, others are little more than "feel good" oases for executives on the rebound.

"EXPANDED RESUME SERVICES"

Avoid this option, or approach it very cautiously. You have probably noticed the advertisements for companies that place "...executives—$25,000 to $500,000..." in the professional positions section of your Sunday paper. Some are legitimate services and can offer a helpful combination of career advice, resume preparation, and industry contacts, but you want to be keenly aware of what you are getting into. Find out exactly what the fees are and what they promise to do for you. Then go home and think about it before you sign the line for several thousand dollars' worth of fancy resume preparation and not much more than you can get from a good book or college placement office.

USING THE INTERNET

Internet job listings are heavily slanted toward high technology and other hard-to-fill job vacancies—much like executive recruiting. With that said, it is still a vast resource for shopping the job market that should not be overlooked. Check the advertised job posting sites, but don't ignore such less obvious possibilities as your college's placement service page. Specific companies also list employment opportunities on their web pages, as do government agencies and other kinds of institutional employers.

Internet Tip

To sample the job search possibilities on the Internet, try: http://www.job-hunt.org/ or enter the keywords "job listings" in your favorite search engine.

The Preliminary Hiring Selection Process

Before the vacancy was ever announced, the people who will interview you for the position decided on how to fill it. They considered everything from eliminating the job and giving the responsibilities to other people, to hiring someone of twice your professional stature. They contemplated

- what the ideal use of the new person would be;
- what missing qualities should be brought in from the outside this time;
- what kinds of flaws the last person had that should be avoided;
- how filling this vacancy will affect the morale of the existing staff; and
- where the new person will fit into the organization.

In-house considerations set the stage for the attitudes you encounter at the interview.

KNOWING THE HIRING SITUATION

The more you know about the background of the hiring, the better able you are to appreciate it and respond appropriately at the interview. For example, you would know why it's important to be sensitive to a division head who fought to eliminate the position, or a manager who wanted a person with more experience than you have for the job.

Learning such things from research and networking help you to have a successful interview. This is not information you find printed in position announcements—it is more apt to reach you via personal contacts on the inside.

Sometimes your challenge comes from the outside. You can encounter a sophisticated interviewing situation created by a consultant brought in especially to shape up internal hiring practices. Writing in *Industry Week*, James Braham quoted an Apple Computer executive who described how his company worked with a consultant to develop "success models" and "behavior profiles" that illustrate "the skills and mechanisms people use to get things done [at Apple]." The consultant stayed on to assist them in structuring their interview questions to get the right information. Some of the information would have come out anyway in the course of routine interview conversations, but the hiring team made sure that the important things were targeted—and that can make for a demanding interview.

While many hirings are still spontaneous, more companies are going to great lengths to define employee qualifications and determine if you possess them during your interview. If you expect that and prepare for it, you will have a leg up on your competition. You will improve your chances of remaining a contender after equally qualified but poorly prepared candidates slip to the background during the important preliminary selection process. Here is a step-by-step look at how a typical hiring develops.

THE POSITION IS ANNOUNCED

You find that most jobs are posted internally for the benefit of present employes. This is a way for a company to make growth opportunities available to its own people. It is also done to encourage employees to refer qualified acquaintances—a way to find you without paying a recruiting or placement fee. You sometimes earn your friend a finder's fee if you prove to be the successful candidate—this is a popular in-house practice that generally costs much less than paying an employment agency. A recruiter is engaged only if the position calls for skills that are not easily found by referral or routine advertising. The recruiter might come from the company's own human resources department or a consulting firm that specializes in the kind of person being sought.

Newspaper and professional publication advertising is used to reach a broad cross section of candidates—often to satisfy equal opportunity hiring requirements. Listings with public employment agencies and college placement offices are also popular approaches for certain levels of hiring and in addition help to substantiate a firm's efforts to hire from a broad pool of applicants. The Internet is also used to post job vacancies to an international audience of millions of potential candidates.

RESUMES, LETTERS, AND APPLICATIONS

How you learned about the vacancy determines what steps you take in applying for it. When a position is announced or advertised by a large organization, you can usually expect to make formal application through the personnel office. The manager you will be working for becomes involved in the process only later. The human resources department screens applicants, sees to it that the company's hiring procedures are followed, and then presents the line manager with a group of "prequalified" candidates from which to choose. Your first point of contact in the interview process is probably going to be a human resources person and not someone from the department where you will be working—that comes after you survive the first cut of the selection process.

RESUME AND COVER LETTER

You need a professional-looking resume that puts you in the most favorable light for the job. While *Resumes That Mean Business, Third Edition* (Random House, 1999) should be your detailed guide to preparing the right resume, here are some important things to keep in mind:

Resume and Cover Letter Suggestions

- Keep your resume brief—one page for most people, two at the most.

- Avoid limiting yourself unnecessarily with a job title or objective that is too narrow (unless you are targeting one highly specific vacancy and are not interested in being considered for related positions).

- Leave the issue of salary for later.

- Select the right resume format for your situation.

  - ✓ *Work History* (or "chronological") if you have a perfect lockstep pattern of employment that leads to the position for which you are applying.

  - ✓ *Focused* (or "targeted") if you are zeroing in on a very specific position and have the qualifications to fill the niche perfectly.

  - ✓ *Competency Cluster* (or "functional") if your talents fall into recognizable and marketable groups of skills. This is the way to sell yourself if you don't want to stress breaks in employment, irregular patterns of experience, etc.

- Use a personal computer and customize your resume to each position.

- Consider your audience—simple enough to be understood by the personnel department, detailed enough to impress a technical manager.

- Include concrete examples of problem-solving and achievement.

- Make your cover letter even more readily understood than your resume by linking your skills to the employer's advertised needs, point for point in a graphic way, such as using "bullets" and short statements in related comparisons (e.g., Your requirement: My qualification that meets it, etc.). One page maximum length.

- Use keywords that are instantly recognizable by human search committees and automated personnel screening systems alike. With large companies, expect to submit a text-formatted resume by e-mail and receive an e-mail acknowledgement early in the screening process.

Part III addresses job search correspondence in greater detail and provides examples of letters.

THE COMPANY APPLICATION FORM

You are expected to complete a company application form so there is a formally signed record of how you represented yourself to the company—your academic background, experience, and answers regarding criminal convictions and substance abuse. Sometimes the application is just a formality that comes late in the hiring process—but that privilege is increasingly limited to higher-level positions or when you have a well-established professional reputation.

When the application comes early in the employment cycle, complete it neatly and thoroughly, and top it off with a personalized cover letter and resume. Address the package to someone specific, and refer to the job for which you are applying. Never use a "to whom it may concern" letter and broad generalities that make it apparent that you are just shipping off another resume. You also create a poor impression when you ask for a position that is not even close to the one advertised or use handwritten strikeouts and corrections to make your old resume fit a new situation. That approach increases your chances for rejection unless you have some truly exotic talent than is in great demand—and most people don't have that luxury.

If you know the name of the hiring official, use it even if you send the package through personnel. Depending on your situation, a "cover letter to your cover letter" may be in order. You need to identify your interviewing audience and cater to everyone involved as you present your credentials. The human resources official will respect your knowledge of who the hiring official is if you make it clear that you are depending on him or her to get your material to that decision maker. If human resources is heavily involved, make an effort to get that contact's name and title correct—and use it—just as you do in the case of your hiring official.

One question on the company application form deserves special attention: salary. If you are asked to enter each job in your work history and the associated salary, give a range (e.g., mid-$40s to upper $50s; or, began lower $30s, left earning in the mid-$40s). When completing the information for your present position, put the beginning salary followed by a dash indicating clearly that the upper limit has not been shown. Another option is to note that present salary will be disclosed at the time of an offer. If asked what your salary requirements are, respond "open" or "negotiable." These salary questions can only hurt you and help the company in salary negotiations when an offer is made. Give them a range so they know they can afford to consider you—that is all they really need to know during the screening phase.

HUMAN RESOURCES, PERSONNEL, AND THE LINE MANAGER

You need to understand the hiring procedure so you can cater to each of the people you will be dealing with. Don't expect the human resources person to know detailed buzz words of a specialized job. He or she will have the big picture, know the general requirements, be oriented toward some firm criteria that have to be met (and a few turnoffs that mean certain rejection), but the nitty-gritty professional discussions come when you meet your working colleagues.

The terms "human resources" and "personnel" are used interchangeably, although human resources is the more contemporary one. In either case, it refers to people, usually in large companies, whose full-time job is to hire, train, and administer benefits to the employees. They work cooperatively with the line managers who actually supervise employees. Personnel is a support function; keep that fact in perspective as you go through the job interview process. Don't lose sight of the fact that it is the line manager who makes the hiring decision and for whom you will ultimately be working.

The relationship between human resources and line managers varies by the company's size and the way it operates. In some firms, managers do their own hiring, and personnel handles the paperwork. In others, human resources has a mandate from top management to keep line managers honest when it comes to everything from equal opportunity compliance and salary guidelines to rigorous screening, interviewing, and background checking.

Your best strategy is to work through personnel, respecting its role, but also try discreetly to establish contact with the person who will eventually hire you. If you are rebuffed and told you have to deal only with human resources, don't press the issue. Wait for the hiring to rise to the working manager's level. On the other hand, if you find the line supervisor receptive to your inquiry, cultivate the linkage and find out as much about the actual requirements as you can. Respect the fact that you don't need any enemies in the hiring chain, and never blatantly bypass anyone. With a little discretion you can keep them all happy and supporting your application.

THE SCREENING PROCESS

THE FIRST SORT

After the deadline for accepting applications has passed, you and the other candidates are sorted into stacks that reflect how well you satisfy the objective requirements. Those who don't have the necessary education and experience are set aside and thanked for their interest. Applicants with too much or the wrong kind of preparation meet a similar fate. Ineptly presented candidates who lack extraordinary talent are bypassed. And those doing the selection eventually settle on a group of applicants who best satisfy the needs of the company on paper. These are ranked, and a small group is selected for further scrutiny—the interviews begin.

TELEPHONE INTERVIEWS

Chances are good that the first round of personal contact will come by telephone. A human resources person will call you and begin the subjective process of determining whether you seem to "fit." There are plenty of objective questions asked, and they certainly matter, but for the first time the hiring process also contains a personal element that can help or hurt your chances of getting the job. This is where your intangible qualities begin to impress those examining you for hiring—warmth, confidence, articulate speech, believable enthusiasm, knowing the language of the business, and the good judgment to say the "right" things.

Saying the Right Things in Your Telephone Interview

- Sound composed and in control even if the call was not expected—sometimes they are prearranged, at other times they come out of the blue from a resume you had sent and forgotten about.

- Have your supporting job search and note-taking materials readily available at the telephone so you can retrieve company information, respond to questions about your resume or application, and take notes during the call.

- Be businesslike but pleasant. Your goal is to command respect and be likable—no first names unless invited, no nervous chewing-gum popping, cigarette lighting, or throat clearing.

- Use the interviewer's questions as opportunities to present your strengths and not just respond to what they ask, but keep it brief.

- Try to learn what they want—the problem to be solved, the job to be done, the personal and professional qualities being sought. Then build your case in response to the needs expressed—now and later.

- Avoid the temptation to ask about salary and benefits. Unless you are literally forced to answer, tap dance if you are asked what your requirements are ("I'm sure XYZ Corporation pays competitive salaries, and we'll have no trouble in that area"). If forced, answer: "My present salary is in the mid-thirties [or whatever], and I would, of course, expect a reasonable incentive above that."

- Get the interviewer's name and title correct, verify the spelling, make notes on everything significant so you can follow up and be well prepared for the face-to-face interview that should follow. Identify other principals, too, if you can do so gracefully (e.g., if talking to the personnel official, get the name of the line manager who will interview and hire you).

- Be ready with a few intelligent questions of your own when the interviewer finishes:

✓ What projects and challenges could you expect to face when you begin?

✓ What qualities does he or she see as crucial to meeting them successfully?

✓ Could we set an appointment for the interview now?

✓ What is the status of the XYZ initiative you read about in the *ABC Journal*? It sounds like a fascinating project! (Use only if your research has provided you with solid information for such questions.)

✓ Where do we go from here? (Push for scheduled, continuing contact—an interview, an invitation to check back in a week or so, at the very least).

✓ Would you mind clarifying something I saw on your Web page? (Be careful not to make this appear contrived; use only if you find something you genuinely would like to know.)

• Say thanks!

• Accept the interview if offered, even if you are less than ecstatic about what you heard—it could be better than you think, it could lead to something else, you can always use the practice and end up saying no.

These are the preliminary rounds of getting the actual face-to-face interview. As you will soon see, there are ways to ease your passage to that point. You can learn things during the preliminaries that will influence your success at the advanced stages of the job interview process.

Finding Out If the Job Is Really Available

The founding editor of a successful national professional newspaper once told me that the financial turning point for his publication was implementation of the Equal Employment Opportunity Act of 1964. Overnight his classified advertising section became the gold mine it remains today. Every employer in the country was placing ads for positions to satisfy affirmative action reporting requirements. A lot of good people were undoubtedly hired as a result, but to no one's surprise, many of the jobs were (and are) advertised when the position had already been filled.

The truth is that many advertised positions are anything but available, and it is naïve to spend your valuable job-hunting energy on someone's compliance drill. One of the first things you need to determine in your job search is whether your interest in the position would be welcomed or merely tolerated. Whether it happens in-house or as the result of a national solicitation, do not let yourself become a "can't win" candidate. Here are a few ways you can sort out the legitimate opportunities.

THE "NO VACANCY" VACANCY

Ask some early questions. There is nothing wrong with inquiring, "Are there any in-house candidates for the position?" And, although you are not apt to be told outright that someone has the job wrapped up, the tone of your discussion may give you insight into how serious the company is about bringing someone in from the outside. Use your network to find out whether the hiring committee is just "kicking tires" to see if there might be someone out there more desirable than their candidate, fleshing out the "we advertised the position" file for a prearranged hire, or whether you would be an honest contender for the job. If you end up with serious doubt about the legitimacy of the opportunity, don't waste your time unless you want interview practice.

CAN YOU HIRE ME IF YOU SELECT ME?

Another question to ask is, "Has this position been funded?" Without the right answer, you could find yourself applying for a job and going through the full screening process only to find that there is no money available to hire you. Find out at the beginning if you are part of some department head's gamble to add a position by the time he or she has advertised and interviewed a batch of candidates.

Just as all advertised positions are not available to everyone who might apply, so every candidate doesn't see his successful job interview turn into employment. Be skeptical enough to determine whether you are competing for a fully funded position before you commit to the application process. Being the darling of the job interview will not count for much if the departmental budget fails to include a line for your salary and benefits.

HOW WILL YOUR APPLICATION AS AN INSIDER BE RECEIVED?

"Genuineness of opportunity" questions are there for you as an in-house candidate, too. Sometimes it is even more difficult to ferret out the monkey drill when you are to be the stalking horse in an internal hiring.

To avoid the problem, you must begin with a candid self-appraisal of your qualifications—especially your status in the political structure that controls the hiring. If the only person openly encouraging your application is the person who is leaving and you know they're glad to see him or her go, that speaks volumes about your chances of success. Sterile, objective responses to your inquiries by those in the hiring chain are another sign that your pursuit of the position is doomed. Most successful inside hires are warmly encouraged, and there are plenty of winks and nods to reinforce faith in your ultimate triumph.

Still, judgment is necessary in deciding what you should do, even when it appears that you are not the chosen one. Often a gracious run for the roses and magnanimous acceptance of defeat leave you nicely positioned for the next time or simply enhance your present desirable status. Not to compete may have branded you lazy and complacent and put your present status at risk. There is also the possibility that the chosen candidate will not accept and you turn out to be the best bet after all. If promotion is critical to your career or ego, plan to move on instead of up in any organization that fails to recognize your potential quickly. If not, go with the flow and enjoy your work while relegating the politics to its rightfully limited place.

Your course of action depends entirely on your objectives, but a little reconnaissance before throwing your hat into your own company's ring can eliminate unpleasant surprises and position you well to deal with realities. One sure career wrecker is to be a poor loser. Appraise your situation realistically, play the role you are given in the circumstances, then prepare to be a magnanimous supporter of the chosen one—or quietly, systematically find a new job.

When to Take the Initiative

There is a fine line between being interested and being a nuisance as the hiring unfolds. You need sensitivity to tell the difference and bring yourself to the attention of the people sorting the candidates at only the right times—and in the right ways. The proper call at the correct time can keep your resume in play just when it was about to head for the circular file. On the other hand, if you overdo it you also risk giving yourself an unwanted nudge toward rejection.

Your initiatives can be classified in two ways:

1. *Reconnaissance.* This is when you call to get general information that could apply to any candidate (e.g., What is the deadline for applications? Is there an in-house candidate? Whom would I report to? What is the spelling of the hiring official's full name? Her (or his) title? Where can I request a copy of your annual report?).

2. *Status checking.* This is when you ask where you personally stand at a particular point in the hiring cycle (e.g., Is my application still under active consideration? Will I be asked to appear for an interview? When will you be making me an offer?).

Reconnaissance questions are generally better tolerated than status checking. There is a distinction made between the conscientious candidate trying to learn all he or she can about the opportunity, and the overly anxious applicant constantly trying to determine where he or she stands. Most employers are prepared to deal with you a reasonable number of times when your questions relate to knowing more about the position. Few companies are willing to tell you where you rank in the pack of interested applicants. Reconnaissance questions can usually be asked of third parties who may know names, positions, and information about the company and the job but who have little involvement in the hiring decision. As you will learn in Chapter 2, these are the people to cultivate when preparing for your interview.

The opportunities for you to express personal interest during the preliminary stages are limited. If you know the people doing the hiring, by all means follow up your application package with a friendly but businesslike call expressing your sincere interest in the position. Offer to make yourself available for questions and to provide additional information if it might be helpful. Once you have done that, excessive communication will detract from your appeal. An exception might be if someone on the inside indicates that the job emphasis has changed or that some aspect of your qualifications is not clearly understood. In such instances a brief follow-up letter to clarify the matter could be both helpful and appropriate.

Networking Your Way to an Interview

Your ability to influence the hiring decision isn't limited to what you can do personally; third parties can also help. A friend employed by the company can put in a good word for you or introduce you to someone involved in the hiring. An influential reference can take an initiative on your behalf instead of your waiting to be called by the employer. Using the knowledge and influence of friends and friends of friends is called "networking," and it can help you get the interview.

Another side of networking involves your laying the groundwork for solid reference checks and inquiries. Employers know that your resume is a personal sales document and that your references are almost certainly going to be favorable ones. They also know that in our litigious society they aren't going to be getting very candid opinions unless they actively seek them. For all of these reasons, expect *employers* to network to find out about *you*.

You should initiate your own contacts within the same group of people and prepare them to respond favorably. Let your former supervisors and colleagues know that they might be contacted, whether or not they have been listed as formal references. Tell them why you feel qualified for and enthusiastic about the position so they can feel motivated to help and mirror your interest. Some interviewers now make it a practice to ask for "negative references"—people you had problems with in an earlier job. Networking can prepare such unlikely "references" for an unexpected call. Whether such an encounter ends up amounting to damage control or actually putting a positive spin on what used to be a strained relationship depends largely on your diplomatic skills before the reference check occurs.

You will learn more about networking in Chapter 2 as you go beyond the preliminary task of getting the interview. For now you must recognize the potential for networking your way to the interview, systematically working the crowd, and seeing that your application is evaluated personally by the people who count. A word to the line manager from a respected colleague can trigger a call to human resources suggesting that you be interviewed. Without that little bit of outside help you might have been relegated to the second round of interviews that often never take place. Your network humanizes the hiring process before you are able to do so yourself. The network call is from someone with a face and a name, a personality and a reputation, a known quantity who ranks above the faceless resumes being sorted down to a reasonable number for interviewing.

Improving Your Odds of Getting an Interview

Remember that your main objective during the preliminary stages of the hiring process is to get the interview. Following are suggested actions to improve your chances of being interviewed. Keep in mind that only you can determine which ones are appropriate to your particular hiring situation. Implemented sensitively and with skill, they can help you get through the door, to where your talents can finally be showcased. Used as obvious gimmicks, they can actually work against you. So before you begin, plan your activities and consider the impact they might have.

BE IN TOWN ON BUSINESS

Interviewing candidates from out of town is costly for companies. One sure way to increase your chances of being on the interview list is to make yourself available at no cost. When you learn that interviews are scheduled for a certain time period and you haven't been invited, a call to the hiring official announcing your availability can sometimes do the trick. Just tell the official you will be in town on business on the same date and have time to schedule an interview. You may have been a second- or third-round interview, but by making it easy for the company to have a look at you along with (or even before) the first-round candidates, you rank yourself a cut or two higher in the selection process and increase your chances of being hired. Case History 2 illustrates this technique.

FAX OR E-MAIL A REVISED RESUME

If you omitted something like a significant course, workshop, or completed degree, or have learned something about the company or the position that lets you recast your qualifications in a more favorable light, take the occasion to send a revised resume. Fax and e-mail add urgency and grab immediate attention. Follow up with a printed copy by mail, but get yourself noticed by sending a time-sensitive update while the selection process is going on. You increase your odds of interviewing because of improved credentials, initiative, and a demonstrated awareness of the impact of current business technology. Take the trouble to make the revision objectively better—not just a ruse to get attention. The fax machine is not always the most private way to communicate, since one often serves the entire office. But with that in mind, use it to get attention and keep your application package up to the minute. E-mail, on the other hand, can be precisely targeted. Make the most of e-mail carbon copies and blind carbon copies to cultivate your network.

HAVE A REFERENCE CALL OR E-MAIL THE INTERVIEWER

You might have a reference listed on your application who is sincerely interested in helping you. Rather than passively wait for a reference check—which often doesn't take place until after you've interviewed and are on the verge of being offered the position—ask your reference to call or e-mail the interviewer to verify if the letter of reference has been received. This can accomplish several things:

- It shows that your reference holds you in high enough regard to go the extra distance for you. But more importantly,
- It sets up an informal reference check before the selections for interviewing have even been made.

Your mentor can take the occasion to speak highly of you and your appropriateness for the position. He or she can also respond to any questions the interviewer has about your qualifications. That little bit of added endorsement might keep you in the "must interview" stack. You can really gain points if the reference has status in your field and is either acquainted with or admired by the hiring official. Your status rises instantly by association. This technique is illustrated in Case History 3.

DO BUSINESS WITH YOUR INTERVIEWER

If you can take an initiative that would put you in legitimate business contact with the person considering your application, do it. There is no better showcase for your talents than doing what you do in real life before the person interested in hiring you. Whether it is a sales call or a professional presentation, nothing surpasses the impact of a de facto "interview" that consists of you and the prospective supervisor actually doing business together. You can't let it look contrived, but you can alter the timing of appointments or trade assignments with a colleague if the result is an opportunity to appear before the hiring official. While you are there, the person should make the connection between the coincidence of your presence and your pending application; if not, find a discreet way to raise the issue and express interest. As in earlier interview-enhancing techniques, you have to use good judgment and walk the fine line between being offensively brazen and being attractively filled with initiative. The technique is illustrated in Case History 4.

Your Interview's Importance to the Employer

The hiring ritual is as full of risk and expense for your employer-to-be as it is for you—sometimes more. At Apple Computer the typical executive hire goes through at least a dozen, and as many as fifteen interviews. According to *Industry Week*, a New Jersey consulting company reported that "...every 100 resumes produce three telephone interviews, or 'screens,' every three screens produce one initial in-person interview, and every six or seven first in-person interviews produce one hire....Each person hired costs an estimated $20,000 in transportation and interviewing expenses." Industrywide studies in the mid-1980s set the cost of hiring at $15,000 when advertising, search fees, travel, and relocation were included. That figure goes higher if the employment contract guarantees six months' salary for a new hire who doesn't work out, or if you count the "opportunity costs" of not having the right person in the job for a period of time. Still more costs occur if in-house morale and effectiveness suffer when an outside choice is made and staff candidates move on because they did not move up. Harry Bacas reported in *Nation's Business* that "half of all new hires stay with a company no more than six months, and each mis-hire can cost 30 to 50 percent above annual salary in lost productivity and the expense of replacement." Finally, a more broadly focused *Fortune* article by Brian Dumaine quotes authorities who place the cost of an unsuccessful hiring at between $5,000 for an hourly worker and $75,000 for a manager.

Regardless of the figure you find believable in your industry and hiring situation, these numbers explain why you are not the only person experiencing anxiety at your job interview. The company and those responsible for your selection have a major stake in things working out right. In getting ready for your interview you can increase your attractiveness by making that job easier for the person facing you across the hiring desk. Do it by presenting him or her with a purposeful, well-informed,

Case History 2—Situation

IN TOWN ON BUSINESS

Background

Sam Wilson works for a small investment firm in South Carolina as a financial analyst. His job search for a career growth opportunity is at a standstill. ❶ Travel funds are tight, and the money center banks interested in his talents are reluctant to fly him in for an interview, concentrating on local applicants instead. ❷ He decides that the next favorable telephone interview that doesn't result in an invitation for a personal visit will be treated differently—even if it costs him money.

Situation

Sam finishes an exciting forty-five-minute telephone interview conversation with Tom Holder, the chief trust investment officer at National Bank in Baltimore. ❸ He wants an equities manager with just the kind of track record Sam is offering. ❹ As they conclude, Mr. Holder says he'll get back to Sam in a week, after he talks with two local candidates he has to interview first. ❺ A few days pass and Tom decides to take the initiative. He calls the man he knows is very interested in him and makes his job easier. ❻ "Mr. Holder, this is Sam Wilson in Charleston—we spoke last week regarding the investment position in your department," Sam begins. "I'm going to be in Baltimore next week on some other business and I wondered if we might be able to get together." ❼ "Yes, I'd like to met you, Sam. What day are you available?" Holder replies. ❽ "Actually, I have some flexibility, since I'm still making the arrangements for the trip. What would be best for you?" Sam asks. "As I mentioned in our earlier conversation, I'm interviewing two local people at the beginning of the week. If you could be here Wednesday afternoon, ❾ we could consider it an interview. I'll be able to involve some of my people then," Holder says.

Conclusion

Sam makes the trip to Baltimore at his own expense, has a very sucessful interview—the chemistry is right—and he goes home confident of getting the offer. ❿ He learns later that he nosed out one of the local guys who would have almost certainly been hired before National Bank would have spent the money to see him in person.

Case History 2—Analysis

IN TOWN ON BUSINESS

General Strategy

Sam can see that he is being placed in the second tier of interviews not by a weak resume or poor performance during the telephone screening, but because it costs the employer money to bring him to his or her city. He decides to make himself available without cost, but doesn't want to come right out and volunteer to pay his own way, afraid he'll appear overly anxious. So he arranges to be in town on other business.

Specific Points

❶ When your interview is in another city, don't be surprised to find the employer reluctant to invite you if he or she has qualified local candidates.

❷ You might have to spend some money on your own travel if you can't honestly arrange a related business trip at a convenient time.

❸ Your qualifications have to be right, but other factors can still keep you from getting the job.

❹ Sam learned what was apt to happen when he was told that local candidates would be interviewed first. If one of them was qualified, Sam would never see an interview.

❺ After giving the employer a chance to call him, Sam took the initiative.

❻ A quick reminder about their favorable telephone interview was followed by the real test of where he stood—making himself available at no cost.

❼ Favorable interviewer response, but with the possibility that the time would not work out.

❽ Put the employer first when possible—his or her choice of day and time.

❾ Confirmation that it's to be more than a courtesy call—Sam has an interview.

❿ He got the job thanks to the fine qualifications he started out with and the quality that only the personal interview his initiative prompted could convey: He had the right chemistry.

Case History 3—Situation

A REFERENCE CALLS THE INTERVIEWER

Background

Ed Masden is a credit manager in the wholesale restaurant supply business with an application pending at one of the fastest-growing companies in the state. He looks good on paper ❶ but doesn't have name recognition in hiring circles. When he sees no interview developing, Ed decides to ask a friend who was already serving as a reference to ❷ intervene discreetly by initiating an unsolicited call on his behalf.

Situation

Ed calls Tim Howe, a longtime ❸ friend and one of the leading credit managers in the state. He ❹ recounts how his application is dead in the water in spite of his fine qualifications and asks for suggestions on how it might be revived to win him the opportunity to impress the company in person. ❺ Tim mentions that he has worked on a number of professional association projects with the person doing the hiring and that he will give her a call. "Cindy! This is Tim Howe calling. Listen, I know you are in the process of hiring a senior credit manager, and ❻ I want to give my active endorsement to someone." ❼ "Tim, I must have a hundred applications for that job, and most of them are good people..." she begins to explain. "I can appreciate that," he continues, "but I'm sure you want to end up with the best person, and I honestly feel strongly about this guy. ❽ Let me tell you a little bit about him." The conversation goes on, and while she recognizes that influence is being brokered, she respects Tim's opinion and, with promises of nothing more, ❾ adds Ed to her list of people who will be interviewed.

Conclusion

Ed achieves his objective. By having a respected member of his profession take an active role, he gets the interview that leads to a rewarding new job. ❿ Without doing something special to relate his excellent professional and personal qualifications, Ed might never have risen from the stack of applicants.

Case History 3—Analysis

A REFERENCE CALLS THE INTERVIEWER

General Strategy

Ed Masden senses correctly that his application is not moving any closer to an interview appointment on the merits alone. He has a reference with the clout and political skills needed to intervene effectively, so he sets the process in motion. All he asks is the chance to be interviewed; no special favors beyond that are requested.

Specific Points

❶ When you know that your qualifications alone are not going to move you to the interview stage in a crowded field of candidates, you need to act.

❷ If you can move the influence of a powerful reference to the front instead of the end of the hiring process, do it.

❸ A friend with professional stature committed to backing your candidacy is an ideal prospect to take an initiative on your behalf.

❹ Make your case for being well qualified and ask nothing more than a chance to be considered seriously for the interview.

❺ Your ideal mentor already knows the hiring official and can trade on an existing relationship instead of reputation alone.

❻ Your advocate should be strong enough to make a straightforward approach to pushing your candidacy.

❼ It doesn't matter that the field is packed; you are well qualified, and all you ask is to be heard in person.

❽ You benefit by having your sterling qualities actively personalized by a respected third party.

❾ Your friend is asking only for a professional courtesy that can be painlessly granted—an interview, not a job.

❿ By getting the interview, you can get the job. Special effort to get that far is worthwhile.

Case History 4—Situation

DOING BUSINESS WITH YOUR INTERVIEWER

Background

Dorothy Ward is an emergency medical technician who wants to teach in her specialty at a local college. ❶ Her efforts to apply have not met with success for several years. ❷ She learns that the present instructor will be leaving at the end of the year and decides to personalize her application by demonstrating her professional talents at the college.

Situation

Dorothy had responded to emergencies at the college on a number of occasions and knows some of the staff. ❸ When she hears that they are planning a career night, she volunteers to represent her profession. Among the preliminaries is a requirement that each participant come for an interview with the dean. ❹ It is an opportunity to screen the participants for desirability and say thanks for helping on a community service basis. Dorothy has her appointment with Dean Grundy and impresses him with her professionalism.

❺ The career night passes successfully, and he contacts her to teach an evening class. ❻ The class showcases her abilities to teach, order materials, add overload students, and process final grades. ❼, ❽ When the full-time position is advertised the next spring, she is an applicant with an already established reputation for competence, initiative, and a strong motivation to serve the students. ❾ While the usual competitive hiring cycle has to be completed, only an extraordinary turn of events will deny Dorothy the position this time—and there is none.

Conclusion

Dorothy takes the trouble to demonstrate her competency to the person she wants to hire her. In this instance there is time to do it over a period of months. ❿ The same effect can be achieved by making an immediate sales call or scheduling a technical consultation in other fields. The objective is to showcase your talents in the setting where they will be used.

Case History 4—Analysis

DOING BUSINESS WITH YOUR INTERVIEWER

General Strategy

Dorothy needs an inside track to get the teaching position she wants. The most effective way to do that is to show the person doing the hiring that she can do the job. She decides to put her professional talents to work at the college without pay. She parlays that into a part-time position, and finally becomes a "known quantity" candidate for the full-time job she really wants.

Specific Points

❶ You need the required talents, but some situations require special strategies.

❷ If you see a vacancy developing, position yourself to be an obvious candidate.

❸ You need an occasion to present yourself, which doesn't have to be a formal working situation.

❹ The right volunteer setting or business call can provide you with a de facto job interview—or at least a foot in the door.

❺ After your initial working contact, try to sustain the relationship if possible.

❻ The impact is particularly strong when you can repeat the work exposure in different settings.

❼ The ideal outcome is to establish a real-world professional bond.

❽ Your efforts pay off when the informal exposure connects with an actual hiring situation for which you are already a known quantity.

❾ You still have to complete a regular competitive hiring, but are positioned as the candidate with the built-in advantage of having been observed and appreciated on a professional level.

❿ If time is short, the same technique works while you are actively under consideration. Arrange to make a business call while your application is pending, and turn the occasion into an invitation for a formal interview.

"self-qualified" candidate. Demonstrate from your first expression of interest to your final response to their questions that you know what they need and are in a position to prove that you can deliver it. Show them a winner they don't have to struggle to understand. Give them reason to believe it's going to be a long time before they have to go through this particular staffing hassle again.

SUMMARY CHECKLIST: GETTING THE INTERVIEW

- Learn everything you can about the hiring situation: who is involved and what are their biases?

- Verify that the position is realistically available to you. Or is it already a "done deal" on which you would be wasting your time?

- Find out if the position is fully funded and that you could begin working right away if selected.

- "Self-qualify" with an honest match of your qualifications to the employer's needs, and increase your odds of interviewing successfully by pursuing only realistic situations.

- Determine the role of human resources and line manager, and craft your application package and personal initiatives to respect all the players while keeping the emphasis on the ultimate decision maker.

- Focus your application on the specific needs of the position for which you are applying. Personal computers make it easy to personalize your resume and letter of application.

- Be prepared for a telephone interview—scheduled or otherwise.

- Be sensitive to the differences between "reconnaissance" initiatives and "status checking" initiatives, and use both to your greatest advantage without wearing out your welcome.

- Discreetly use your networking capabilities to learn what is going on in the mind of the hiring official, and make him or her aware of your interest through third parties, if that can be done effectively.

- Use networking to prepare your references (even a few "negative" ones) for a possible call from the employer.

- Implement your own strategies for increasing your odds of getting the interview if you are not scheduled for one early in the hiring cycle.

- Appreciate the importance of the interview to the employer, and do your part to make it worthwhile for both parties.

2 PREPARING FOR THE INTERVIEW

Whether you already have an interview scheduled or are still trying to arrange one, you have some preparing to do. The knowledge you gain in the process helps you in either situation—(1) by being impressive enough during the preliminary selection process to get the interview or (2) by doing well enough when you face your interviewer to get the job. You make your preparations with a four-part approach that involves learning about:

- sources of information;
- the company and its people;
- what you want and what you have to offer; and
- the interview process and how you can influence it.

The four approaches blend and overlap, but the knowledge that you gain in each strengthens your overall preparation for the job interview. Your objective is to learn as much as you can about the information sources for the position you are pursuing, the company and the people working for it, your own talents and what you expect from your career, and what you are apt to encounter as you move through the job interview process.

You are going to use information that is all around you but may not have mattered to you until now. Everyday sources, none of them created with your particular job search in mind, become useful and make you a more successful candidate once you become aware of their potential. Some of your sources are passive—books on the shelves of libraries. Others are active—people you'll contact, places you'll go,

GETTING THE INTERVIEW
- Finding a job
- Applying
- Networking
- Getting invited

PREPARING FOR THE INTERVIEW
- Researching the company
- Preparing personally
- Anticipating questions

You get ready for your interview by becoming informed about the company in order to be a knowledgeable candidate and to evaluate the desirability of working for it. You must first convince yourself that you are the best person for the job in order to convince others with your confidence, knowledge, and motivation. Next you prepare yourself for the interview process by knowing questions you are likely to encounter. Finally, you get ready to ask some questions yourself. Impress the interviewers with your informed interest and also learn about the promise and problems of the working situation.

APPEARING FOR THE INTERVIEW
- Reconnaissance
- Personal readiness
- Timing

DURING THE INTERVIEW
- Names and personalities
- Style and substance
- Satisfying agendas

LEAVING THE INTERVIEW
- Reading your audience
- Positive expectations
- Last impression

EVALUATING YOUR INTERVIEW
- Substantive match
- Personal chemistry
- Judging your chances

FOLLOWING UP AFTER YOUR INTERVIEW
- Thank you's
- Additional information
- More networking

CONCLUDING THE INTERVIEW PROCESS
- The offer
- Negotiating
- Accepting

Figure 2. Preparing for the Interview.

and information you'll come across while aggressively researching a company on the Internet.

Before getting into the specifics of preparing for your interview, look at the whole process and see where it is leading you. Understand that what you are about to do in "Preparing for the Interview" continues steps that you began in Chapter 1, "Getting the Interview." Look ahead on the job interview continuum and see how valuable your preparation is going to be as you move through the job interview cycle.

Sources of Information

The information you need comes from many sources, including community organizations; regional and national publications; the Internet; and, among the most valuable, your network of friends and professional acquaintances. The following selective list is an overview of the kinds of resources that can make you a better-informed job candidate. Use this as a starting point for your own imaginative search for print and electronic publications and people who can tell you what you need to know about your job opportunity.

Internet Tip

Many information sources have their own web pages. For example: http://www.bbb.org will link you to individual Better Business Bureaus and at http://www.chamber-of-commerce.com you can find Chambers of Commerce all over the world. Enter a business reference, company or newspaper name, or other keywords that interest you into Metacrawler.com or your favorite search engine for results that may be of particular value to you.

BETTER BUSINESS BUREAU

The Better Business Bureau (BBB) is listed in your telephone book. If you are investigating a company in another part of the country, check the library for that city's telephone directory, call long distance directory assistance, or ask your local BBB for a referral. Don't expect an elaborate report when you call, but what you get will be useful. The spokesperson checks to see if the company you ask about has been the subject of complaints from customers and clients, and she or he will discuss the general nature of any problems with you. The BBB representative will not recommend whether you should work for the firm, of course. Finding a company with a derogative file should be a red flag to you—dig deeper to find out whether this is the kind of organization you want to be affiliated with, depend on for a living, or add to your resume.

CHAMBERS OF COMMERCE

Most cities have a Chamber of Commerce office. It is an advocate for the local business community and an excellent source of basic information on the company you are investigating. The Chamber of Commerce is listed in the telephone book and is usually located in a community's business district. You can purchase an inexpensive directory of members that includes almost every enterprise in the area, public and private. Each company pays dues to belong, and the directory tells you how many employees it has, what it does, how long it has been in business, and whom to contact for more information. Regional directory companies publish a more extensive guide, and you can examine a copy at the chamber office or library. In addition to information on your prospective employer, the Chamber of Commerce can also help you evaluate the community as a place to live and work.

The chamber staff is usually well informed on regional trends and personalities. Start a discussion about the company that interests you and see what they have to say. You might learn of plans to expand or close the plant, for example. Think about what you would like to know, and ask. Interesting tidbits about company executive officers can often be picked up from people who meet them socially. Ask what kind of reputation your prospective employer has as a place to work—you usually get an honest opinion if you ask in the course of a casual conversation. A written inquiry will probably get you a list of members, a local map, and maybe a community brochure for your trouble. But you have to dig for what you really want to know. Visit the office personally or, at a minimum, telephone and put the force of your personal interest behind your inquiry.

CREDIT CHECK

If you are looking for information on an established, midsize business, you can see how the company rates in *Dun & Bradstreet* or *Moody's* by checking the reference section of your library. Both references tell you whether the company is considered to be a good credit risk, and that, of course, indicates something of its overall strength and character. If you are considering a position with a small organization or an individually owned firm, the same kind of credit bureau that rates your personal credit rates theirs. You may need a business or legal connection to get a report, but if you are concerned about the firm's financial stability, pursue the matter with your attorney, who can either get the information or advise you on how to do it ethically. Credit bureau reports are not routinely available to individuals, but there are ways to get the information if you have a legitimate need to know.

You can also ask your prospective employer for banking and accounting references to verify the condition of the company. While these are usually perfunctory contacts that tell you little more than that the firm is a client, it can uncover a "worst case" scenario if the organization is on the verge of disaster. For example, you can ask if the company appears to be sound financially. A hedged answer is an invitation to look more closely. Standard business references list the professional and financial affiliations of major companies; you have to ask smaller companies for the names of their accounting and law firms and their banks. If they refuse, consider it to be a red flag, and investigate further before you make a career commitment.

Credit checks are not needed in many job searches, but they are a reasonable precaution if you sense there might be problems. You don't want to end up like a major hotel chain executive who recently accepted a high-level position, relocated his family, purchased a new home, and was soon informed that his position had been eliminated to meet financial exigencies. You can spare yourself the career disruption by checking the financial health of your employer-to-be ahead of time.

STANDARD BUSINESS REFERENCES

Thomas' Register of American Manufacturers, Standard & Poor's Register of Corporations, Directors and Executives, MacRae's Bluebook, and others geared to specific industries or regions of the country can help you determine what a company does, the scope of its operations, its business affiliations, the names of officers heading its major divisions, and much more. For other sources, ask your librarian or call a local college professor teaching in your field—he or she will usually point you in the right direction and be complimented that you asked. Here is a sampling of what can be found in *Standard & Poor's Register* (adapted from *User's Companion to Poor's Register*):

✓ accounting firm

✓ address

✓ affiliates

✓ bank (primary)

✓ directors (including personal information)

✓ divisions

✓ employees (number of)

✓ executives (including personal information)

✓ law firms

✓ officers (including personal information)

✓ personnel (key)

✓ products

✓ sales (annual)

✓ services

✓ Standard Industrial Classification (SIC) codes

✓ stock exchanges (where traded)

✓ subsidiaries

✓ telephone number

PUBLISHED INDEXES AND COMPUTER DATABASES

Magazine, newspaper, and professional journal indexes give you leads to articles about companies and the people who run them. Libraries have computer terminals for accessing databases. Use them to find information on the company, its products, people, and competitors—the industry itself. Try entering the name of your interviewer or industry personalities—one of them may have just published an article or given a speech that made the trade news. Maybe your human resources contact wrote something for a personnel journal. Reading it could give you insight into how he or she will deal with you—and present you with an opportunity both to compliment him or her and demonstrate your awareness of the industry. Some computer indexes catalog the speeches of leading business personalities. Locate a few that apply to your specialty and you have the makings of informed, businesslike conversation during your interviews. This kind of "knowledge initiative" impresses employers in an era where finding and using information is increasingly important. The Internet also contains useful current and recent past information, but don't expect to find many free library-grade archives there.

Internet Tip

To examine a fee-based research service try http://www.elibrary.com for Electric Library or enter the keywords "research service" in your favorite search engine to locate other choices.

COMPANY INFORMATION

Public relations departments will answer your questions and mail you information such as annual reports. You may actually be *expected* to familiarize yourself with such publications before your interview. Annual reports are also often available in the business section of the library or at your placement office.

You read them to learn what companies do, what they take pride in doing especially well, what they plan for the future—and to get a flavor for their corporate culture. Pride in a childcare program for its employees might be noted, for example. The company's attitude toward the environment will often be stated. Where the firm sees itself in ten years is a regular feature of such publications.

Annual reports are free public information that tell you a lot about where the company stands, where it hopes to go, and how you might make a contribution. You can also get financial and compliance reports from regulatory agencies.

Candidates entering interviews today must be thoroughly familiar with the company's Web page. Information of every description is found there: Mission statements and objectives; news, leadership, and personalities; investor information and financials; organization charts and annual reports; planned initiatives, and much more. Little things like recognizing key people from their photographs on the company web page can subtly change an interview for the better.

NETWORKING

After you have exhausted your formal sources and know where to begin, get more personal. Talk with people. Finding them is the function of your network. When you network correctly, one contact leads to another until you learn what you need to know. You will see examples of networking used in specific situations throughout this book.

The Company and Its People

The information you need to know depends on the position you are pursuing. If you are going into general management, your interests are wide-ranging and you want the big picture. You need to know about the different operating divisions of the company, but not in-depth. On the other hand, if you are going to work in a specialized part of a firm, your interests will be focused, and you need just enough overall company knowledge to be informed about and appreciate the role your division plays.

Regardless of whether your needs are for broad or focused information, the accompanying chart will start you thinking of the kinds of questions you want to pursue, why they are important to you, and where you can find the answers. Researching them helps you decide whether the opportunity is worthwhile and, if it is, understand both what your interviewers' questions mean and how to respond.

THINGS YOU WANT TO KNOW ABOUT THE COMPANY		
What You Want to Know	**Why You Want to Know It**	**How You Can Find Out**
What does the company do?	• To be a knowledgeable candidate • To decide whether you want to be a part of such an enterprise • To judge future opportunities	• Annual reports • Chambers of Commerce • Library business references • Internet • Network contacts
Who owns the company and what other companies does it own?	• To be a knowledgeable candidate • To avoid overlapping applications and references • To judge its strength and character • To judge future opportunities	• Annual reports • Library business references • Internet • Network contacts
How big is the company?	• To be a knowledgeable candidate • To judge the strength of the company • To judge future opportunities	• Annual reports • Chambers of Commerce • Library business references • Internet
What kind of image does the company have?	• To be a knowledgeable candidate • To decide whether you want to be a part of such an enterprise • To judge its strength and character	• Journals, periodicals, and newspapers • Better Business Bureau • Chambers of Commerce • Credit checks • Internet • Network contacts
Who runs the company?	• To be an informed candidate	• Annual reports

(cont'd)

What You Want to Know	Why You Want to Know It	How You Can Find Out
Who runs the company? *cont'd*	• To judge its strength and character	• Chambers of Commerce • Library business references • Journals, periodicals, and newspapers • Internet • Network contacts
Is the company in trouble?	• To be a knowledgeable candidate • To judge the strength of the company • To judge future opportunities	• Chambers of Commerce • Library business references • Credit checks • Internet • Journals, periodicals, and newspapers • Internet • Network contacts
How does the company's future look?	• To be a knowledgeable candidate • To judge the strength of the company • To judge future opportunities	• Annual reports • Chambers of Commerce • Credit checks • Library business references • Journals, periodicals, and newspapers • Internet • Network contacts
Has the company been in the news recently?	• To be a knowledgeable candidate	• Chambers of Commerce

(cont'd)

What You Want to Know	Why You Want to Know It	How You Can Find Out
Has the company been in the news recently? *cont'd*	• To decide whether you want to be a part of such an enterprise • To judge future opportunities	• Journals, periodicals, and newspapers • Internet • Network contacts
What are the company's products or services?	• To be a knowledgeable candidate • To decide whether you want to be a part of such an enterprise • To judge future opportunities	• Annual reports • Chambers of Commerce • Library business references • Journals, periodicals, and newspapers • Internet • Network contacts
Should I be aware of the reputation and accomplishments of anyone working for the company?	• To be a knowledgeable candidate • To decide whether you want to be a part of such an enterprise • To judge future opportunities	• Annual reports • Chambers of Commerce • Library business references • Journals, periodicals, and newspapers • Internet • Network contacts
What is my interviewer's name, title, and place in the company's organization?	• To be a knowledgeable candidate	• Formal company contacts • Internet • Network contacts
What is my interviewer's background?	• To be a knowledgeable candidate	• Library business references

(cont'd)

What You Want to Know	Why You Want to Know It	How You Can Find Out
What is my interviewer's background? *cont'd*		• Chambers of Commerce • Internet • Network contacts
Is it a smoking or non-smoking organization?	• To determine whether you fit this aspect of the corporate culture	• Formal company contacts • Internet • Network contacts
What are the social expectations for my position?	• To determine whether you fit this aspect of the corporate culture	• Formal company contacts • Network contacts
How much business travel is involved?	• To determine whether you fit this aspect of the corporate culture	• Formal company contacts • Network contacts

APPLYING THE NETWORKING TECHNIQUE

Some of the most useful information comes through networking. Much of it happens while comfortably interacting with your colleagues in routine business and social settings. That's the easy part. But to push beyond that and open up new sources, you have to do what is referred to in sales as "cold calling":

- Your network acquaintances mention others who probably know what you need to find out.
- They suggest that the person would be willing to talk with you.
- Some introduce you to the source or tell you to mention their names to break the ice.

Asking for something from someone you don't know—cold calling—can be unnatural and stressful. Still, it's worth the discomfort because it opens up opportunities not available to your competitors who never network beyond their own comfortable circle of friends and acquaintances. Extend yourself, and your broadened base of contacts will improve your odds of having a successful interview. In the process you open up the possibility of finding opportunities that you might not have even been aware of otherwise. The technique is illustrated in Case History 5.

Case History 5—Situation

> # COLD CALLING WITH LEADS AND
> # INTRODUCTIONS

Background

Pat Lyle is a graphics artist who has developed new abilities in the computer graphics side of her profession. **❶** Most of her contacts, however, are in the traditional pen-and-ink firms. She needs to find a place for her newly developed and highly marketable skills and network a new group of people. **❷** Her few acquaintances in the specialty authorize her to use their names freely but are too busy to help actively. She needs to take the initiative personally.

Situation

Pat gets the **❸** directory issue of her professional journal and identifies people positioned to help her in the kinds of firms she seeks to join. She compares the names to those provided by her friends who agree to vouch for her. **❹** With her list of prospects, she makes calls to people she doesn't know but whose help she needs. **❺** "Good morning Mr. Wilson, this is Pat Lyle. I'm a graphics artist with eight years of experience with Sun Graphics. I've been taking courses in computer graphics, and I'm looking for a position that can use my skills. **❻** Mike Barrett said to mention his name and ask if you might help steer me in the right direction. He says you have a strong computer graphics operation and would know about opportunities if anyone would." Wilson responds that he doesn't anticipate any openings, **❼** but suggests that she call Mary Chun at Island Graphics—**❽** and say that he suggested calling. Pat places the call and finds that Mary is indeed interested in talking with her. She is thinking of advertising a position in a few months and welcomes a viable candidate. **❾** They have an informal interview, Mary suggests a few other possibilities, but Pat accepts a position with her a few months later.

Conclusion

Pat takes the trouble to meet people at the working level in her new field before their needs are advertised. A colleague's reputation helps break the ice and position her to **❿** get a job for which she would have been just another routine candidate had she not taken the initiative.

Case History 5—Analysis

COLD CALLING WITH LEADS AND INTRODUCTIONS

General Strategy

Pat knows that she lacks the contacts to break into the computer graphics side of the business. Her few friends in a position to help are too busy to take an initiative for her, but are willing to have their names used. She uses that little bit of assistance and parlays it into a job by getting on the telephone and finding out where the vacancies are developing.

Specific Points

❶ When you have talent but lack the personal contacts to make them work in a new setting, you need to identify people at the working level who might appreciate what you have to offer.

❷ Mutual professional acquaintances can make cold calling easier.

❸ Your industry almost certainly has a professional directory that identifies people to call in your specialty. If not, call the company and ask who does your kind of work there.

❹ Coordinate your lists and start calling the people who are most apt to be responsive because of an even remotely shared acquaintance.

❺ You need a short script that will pitch your strengths in a brief introduction.

❻ Take advantage of name-dropping and increase your chances of getting helped by someone who might say no to you, but not you *and* a friend.

❼ Cold calls that generate leads are the next best thing to job offers.

❽ Always try to keep the linkage of third-party referrals going—ask to use his or her name when you call the person he or she suggested.

❾ You have succeeded in finding someone who needs you.

❿ Your cold-calling initiative got you the interview and a favorable predisposition to hire before the vacancy was even advertised. The same technique works when trying to find inside information about a job for which you have already made an application—instead of an opening, ask for information.

APPLYING THE "CONSULTANT" TECHNIQUE

When you don't have leads and introductions, you can always call in the capacity of a "consultant." This is a telephone technique for uncovering useful information. While you should never use the technique unethically (blatantly misrepresenting yourself, for example), don't be afraid to talk with people inside the company you want to join. If you don't have an individual's name, just ask to speak with someone who is knowledgeable about your specialty. Such conversations can lead to everything from vacancies that have yet to be announced to an insider's perspective on a position for which you've already applied.

Avoid using your name, since that might prejudice a future interview. If asked, just respond that you are an independent consultant with an interest in conducting your inquiry confidentially. That will satisfy most people. In fact, few ever ask. If you approach them correctly, people will gladly share information. Be businesslike—have your objectives in mind, pursue them professionally, and respect your source's time. You can conduct yourself in such a way as to probe and find out what you need to know without ever being dishonest or saying anything you wouldn't have said in person. Remember that many businesses routinely use "caller ID" and note the telephone number of the calling party. Never *rely* on your call being an anonymous one, but unless you anger someone, a brief call made in confidence remains simply that. Case History 6 illustrates the technique.

Evaluating What You Have to Offer

When the time comes for your interview, you want to focus attention on your strengths. You do that by building your knowledge about the company's needs and your qualifications into a solid case for why the hiring will be good for the company and you. Spontaneous responses alone might not accomplish that goal during your interview. You need to think through the possibilities and make decisions ahead of time. Here are some questions that will help you do that. You should expand the list to cover other topics that define a mutually beneficial relationship between you and your prospective employer.

EVALUATING YOUR POTENTIAL RELATIONSHIP WITH THE COMPANY	
The Company	**And You**
What does the company need?	Do you offer those skills, and are you interested in applying them in this kind of situation?
Will you be in the mainstream or in a support function?	Does it matter to you and your future that you have the potential to reach the top, or is a solid supporting position satisfactory?
What does this company do?	Do you feel good about it, and can you get enthusiastic about being part of the effort? Would you be proud of your work, feel good about telling others what you do and comfortable having it on your resume in the future?
What kind of people succeed in this company?	Do you see yourself as "that kind of person"? Can you identify with the values and behavior of the people who are the visible winners?
Where are the growth opportunities in this company?	Do your skills and personality fit, and is the division to which you are applying an integral part of the company's future growth?
What kind of training or staff development program does the company have?	Will you be helped or hindered as you pursue further education and professional growth? Will you be viewed as doing the right thing, or diluting your efforts for the company? Do you care?
Who will the company be competing with in the course of your time with them?	Are you picking a winner, or are you joining a company that will be bowing to the competition?
What are the growth and profitability histories for the company? What are the projections?	Are you joining a company with solid financial prospects?

Case History 6—Situation

COLD CALLING WITHOUT LEADS AND INTRODUCTIONS

Background

Marla Oakton is an account executive with a midsize brokerage firm and is applying for a position with a large one. ❶ She knows the job description and projected earnings, but before deciding wants to confirm things about the corporate culture—especially the attitude toward women. This kind of information isn't put in writing or honestly discussed at formal interviews.

Situation

❷ Marla knows she needs to talk to her counterparts in a candid and nonthreatening way. Testing company practices that relate to sensitive issues calls for informal, confidential conversations. ❸ She uses her industry directory to identify men and women, account executives and managers, to call. ❹ It won't work to say "Hi, my name is Marla Oakton, a candidate for a position in your company, and I want to know if women are treated professionally and have a fair shot at senior management positions." She knows that a more subtle approach will serve her purposes better. ❺ She starts calling in the capacity of a consultant doing a survey of the industry. ❻ She promises anonymity and asks for it in return; to her surprise, her terms are almost universally accepted.

❼ Callers give their candid impressions on the questions that are of interest to her. ❽ When she finishs, Marla has a broad, candid survey of attitudes on a sensitive subject ❾ that matters greatly in her career decision. She approachs the subject as directly as the realities of current social conditions in the workplace permit—and does nothing dishonest.

Conclusion

Without direct referrals, Marla is able to get inside her future workplace and determine whether prevailing attitudes will suit her needs. ❿ She acts ethically by doing nothing more than creating the circumstances of confidential inquiry needed to gain essential career information for her private use.

Case History 6—Analysis

COLD CALLING WITHOUT LEADS AND INTRODUCTIONS

General Strategy

Marla decides not to risk a career move to an organization that holds traditional attitudes toward the advancement of women. She wants to have honest conversations up front before making a final decision. So she identifies future colleagues and telephones them to survey their attitudes on things that matter to her professionally.

Specific Points

❶ There are issues that cannot be judged accurately by such traditional sources as job descriptions and structured, official conversations.

❷ You sometimes need to talk candidly about private things before deciding to pursue employment in a particular organization.

❸ Most professions have directories that let you identify the people you should be talking with for certain kinds of information.

❹ Ideally, you can raise any issue in an open conversation. Practically, you cannot. This hypothetical lead-in demonstrates how naive it might be.

❺ Anyone can rationalize being a consultant—even working for oneself.

❻ Confidentiality is standard operating practice in business conversations and is easily invoked for your own purposes.

❼ People will generally try to help you; try asking sincere, reasonable questions and see for yourself.

❽ Nothing compares with direct, confidential calling for finding out what you need to know.

❾ Callers sense a valid inquiry; this one had conspicuous relevancy for the caller, and that eased her way in getting useful responses.

❿ Ethical approaches to sensitive issues are very important. In this case nothing was misrepresented, and only the caller used the information.

The Interview Process and Your Influence on It

You might find yourself in one or more of several job interview environments. By knowing what to expect, you can avoid being surprised or intimidated. You are dealing more with variations in technique than substance in different interview formats, and if you are well prepared, are a good fit for the position, and know what is coming, you will be able to impress interviewers regardless of their approach.

You need to know the interviewer's technique and how that applies to you. An aggressive natural leader and a good team player may show very different traits and each still walk away with a successful interview—depending on what the interviewer wants. To make your strongest case, you need to know what is expected, decide whether you can honestly provide it, then deliver it effectively, using your knowledge of the company and what the interviewer is trying to accomplish.

The accompanying table lists different types of interviews. Most interviews are a combination of the following techniques:

- A telephone interview might be either structured or informal—or a hybrid mix of the two.

- A face-to-face interview might be with an individual or a group.

- The interview may require a meeting with a formal panel, and it may or may not incorporate stress to reveal your character.

- The same is true of the interview's purpose—whether screening, selection, or hiring, it could be

  ✓ informal or structured;

  ✓ in person or by telephone (or satellite or computer, for that matter); and

  ✓ individual or group.

Your best strategy is to be aware of the possibilities and then play your role as comfortably as you can. While you should never smile smugly and indicate that you know *exactly* what is going on, you can put aside the stress that being surprised might have brought on and concentrate on being a poised, well-informed candidate.

TYPES OF INTERVIEWS	
Interview Type	**Description/Purpose**
Face-to-face	Interviewer and candidate physically present at the same site for personal interaction.
Group	Candidates are put into a group situation to see how they react in a common task. Leaders and team players emerge.
Hiring	Purpose is to make the offer and negotiate terms of employment.
Informal	Nondirective; interviewer serves more as a moderator; purpose is to bring out the interviewee's personality.
Panel	Also called a "board" interview. A number of interviewers evaluate a single candidate. Example: a college president being selected by a panel consisting of faculty, administrators, and the governing board.
Remote	Telephone, satellite, videotape, computer—an interview where the interviewer and candidate do not encounter each other personally.
Screening	Purpose is to narrow the choices. Weed out anyone with less than complete qualifications or a flaw—look for a reason to reject candidates. Impersonal, fact-oriented, to assess qualifications. Conducted by a human resources specialist using formal interviewing techniques and strategies. Candidate initiative not a good idea—respond to what you are asked, and don't provide a reason to be judged unlikable or inappropriate. Not a time to introduce controversy.
Selection	Purpose is to pick the person to hire—look for a reason to accept the candidate. Intuitive, personal, professional task-oriented. Conducted by a line manager or supervisor often not paying much attention to interview techniques. Candidate should use interview preparation to good advantage. Impress interviewer with job knowledge, personality, skills needed for the actual job.

(cont'd)

Interview Type	Description/Purpose
Situational	Individual is put in a hypothetical situation and asked to resolve it. A one-person variation of the group interview.
Stress	Purpose is to challenge the candidate's opinions and qualifications; use silence to make her or him uncomfortable; curt responses; staring for effect. Onset and end of stress segment are usually apparent—change of interviewer's character and approach.
Structured	Checklist interview where the routine is set and you respond to preconceived questions—no room for spontaneity by interviewer or candidate.

Next in your preparation comes an awareness of what you can expect from your interviewer if he or she follows the traditional rules provided below. The interviewer can be expected to have these ground rules in mind when trying to get to know you. Remember the rules as you prepare for your interview. They tell you where your interviewer is coming from and what he or she is trying to do at various stages of your interview.

Rules the Interviewer Follows

- **Works from a job description**—expect your interviewer to have a list of the job duties, qualifications, and work experience needed.

- **Relaxes the candidate**—your interviewer will make some small talk and ask something about your personal interests to make you feel comfortable.

- **Has an interview schedule**—your interviewer can be expected to move through phases that go from telling you about the position, to examining your background and motivations, to ending with asking for your questions about the position.

- **Listens more than talks**—your interviewer will stress getting you to express yourself and provide information, trying to avoid filling the time with his or her own comments.

- **Conducts a truthful and legal interview**—your interviewer will try to keep his or her comments about the company honest and avoid asking you questions prohibited by equal opportunity regulations.

- **Inquires about salary**—your interviewer may inquire about your salary history but will probably avoid any definitive discussion of anything but the salary range until the time of an offer.

- **Gives the next step**—your interviewer should conclude the interview by making you aware of what comes next in the hiring cycle.

According to an expert quoted in Harry Bacas's *Nation's Business* article on hiring, you can expect the interviewer to "...find out whether [you] can *do* the job; whether [you] *will* do the job the way [the company] wants it done; and whether [you] *fit* into [their] organization."

The interviewer comes to the interview with a plan. Some are very thoroughly prepared; others are less formal and give the appearance of just wanting to get to know you. Nearly all of them have some standard questions that you should anticipate. You don't want to be ready with tape-recorderlike responses, but you should be ready with a well-reasoned, natural answer to the questions that follow.

QUESTIONS YOUR INTERVIEWER MIGHT ASK	
Question	**Suggested Response**
Can you answer this question the way you think your references will answer it?	An implied notice that your response will be verified. Welcome the challenge and suggest asking a certain person to corroborate.
Aren't you overqualified?	You won't waste time training me. Use company knowledge to show you know where you'd fit in if hired. Imply that rapid growth will take care of any problem with overqualification.
Could you give me some references that you didn't get along with?	Be ready. Have a few people in mind who differed with you but with whom you learned to share a mutual respect. Prepare these references for possible contact.
Have you ever had more to do than you could accomplish? How did you handle it?	Yes, you have, and you solved the problem by setting priorities and negotiating new terms when you had to.

(cont'd)

Question	Suggested Response
How did you accomplish that (...some specific thing you claim to have done)?	Be ready to back your claim with demonstrable proof that you did it; be able to talk in specific, operational terms.
How long would it take you to make a contribution here?	Be realistic, but offer an attractive hypothetical accomplishment based on your research, if the situation lends itself.
How much did you save the company when you implemented your new procedure?	Do your homework—have the figures and suggest that they can be verified by checking with a reference.
How much money do you need?	Try to turn the tables; ask what they pay for similar positions. Or you'd like as much as your experience would qualify you for—confident that they'll be fair.
In what area have you shown your greatest improvement in the past two years?	This question is designed to get you to admit a shortcoming and, hopefully, show growth in overcoming it. Try to have a favorable example in mind.
Is there something in your past that you feel less than proud of that you'd rather discuss now than have us discover later?	Don't do your best to come up with something bad to satisfy the question, but if there was an incident that is apt to come to light, say so. Give it as brief and positive a mention as you can.
Name three accomplishments that you are most proud of.	Be ready with some good examples, including how your accomplishments helped others, including your last employer.

(cont'd)

Question	Suggested Response
Name three things you like about your job and three things you don't like about it.	Accentuate the positive, minimize the negative. Acceptable negatives include limited opportunity for growth, desire to take on a new challenge, maturing priorities that called for a change professionally.
Tell me about your faults.	Don't overdo the honesty here—something like "I work too hard..." is fine if you elaborate a little and make it more than a glib response. Don't feel obligated to give them reasons to eliminate you.
Tell me about your professional experience.	Keep it brief and don't make yourself appear too narrow and specialized. Let the interviewer ask for more detail.
Tell me about...(open-ended question)	These questions are to keep you from responding yes or no. Be prepared to explain something briefly.
That sounds great! Were there any negatives?	Sure there were, and mention some minor things, but stress that they were outweighed by the positives.
What are you looking for in this position?	Stay general enough to fit what the company may need. Don't make it more than they can deliver.
What do you and your current supervisor fight about?	"We don't fight—we discuss our differences, I make my views known, and he or she has the ultimate authority—which I respect."
What do you know about our company?	A brief, positive response based on your research that shows you know what they do and their position in the industry. Be ready to go into more detail if asked.

(cont'd)

Question	Suggested Response
What do you think you could contribute to our firm?	Match your skills to the company's needs.
What is the name of the person you reported to in that particular situation?	Have your references ready. A typed list in your briefcase is a good idea. You can produce it when asked.
What is your management style?	Eclectic—you do what works in the situation, but you are results-oriented. Don't name some single style—it might not fit, and most people are indeed eclectic and adaptive.
What qualities do you like in a boss?	If you honestly can, reflect the qualities you see in your interviewer, or generalize and express admiration for the supportive, cooperative manager who will let you grow and set a positive example for you.
What was it about your work that made your supervisor rate you as a good manager?	Operational specifics are what the interviewer wants to hear—not vague generalities. Tell the interviewer about a problem you solved.
What's your worst weakness?	Generalize your response and never give reasons that might be the basis for rejection. "Oh, I guess we all could do a little better at....Actually, it's something I've worked on for the last few years with pretty good results."
Where do you see yourself in five years?	"If the opportunity with this company is what I believe it to be, I'll be right here, moving up the career ladder."
Who benefited from your accomplishments? How?	"My department and company benefited, and here's how....I was also rewarded personally by...."

(cont'd)

Question	Suggested Response
Why did you leave (a previous position)?	Be honest and stay positive. If it was a bad experience and you left under unfavorable conditions, say so, take responsibility, and explain how you've grown as a result.
Why do you switch jobs so often?	Minimize the changes by citing broad experience gained, purposeful progression, and a desire to reach a point quickly where you can stabilize your career—now, with this company.
Why do you want to be part of this organization?	A response that shows realistic ambition and identification with what the company does.
You brought the production figures up to record levels in six months?	This is the "echo question" used by the interviewer to seek more detail. Pick up on the question and establish how you did it.

Have your own agenda when you enter the interview. Granted, the interviewer is in charge, but you have a lot of influence over what the substance of the interview ends up being. You do that to a degree by *answering* questions, but you really accomplish it with the questions you ask.

QUESTIONS YOU MIGHT ASK YOUR INTERVIEWER	
Questions to Ask	**Why You Want to Know**
Well, where do we go from here? Whom will I be seeing next?	These questions will give you some indication whether you are finished or will be moving on up the interview chain; look for body language, enthusiasm, discomfort.

(cont'd)

Questions to Ask	Why You Want to Know
How many people work in this department?	To determine its importance in the overall organization and your relative status in the company.
Exactly where do I fit into the organization?	To learn the role you will play relative to others and to attach real meaning to your job title and description.
To whom do I report, and what are the overall reporting relationships within the department?	This is another way to determine your true status.
Who reports to me, and what does that mean in terms of authority?	This defines your status and power relative to others in the organization.
How important is this division to senior management?	To judge whether you can get noticed there by higher-ups.
How do you see this company developing over the next few years?	To judge your opportunities for growth.
What are your plans for expansion that would affect my future?	To judge your opportunities for growth.
How would you describe the working relationship between this division and senior management?	To establish whether you will be interacting with the leaders directly or screened by others.
How would you describe the management style here?	To see if you fit.
Why did my predecessor leave?	To see if there was a problem that you might have as well—maybe a pattern of people not being able to succeed in the position.

(cont'd)

Questions to Ask	Why You Want to Know
How long has this position been open?	To determine whether others are finding good cause to reject the opportunity; if they're having trouble filling it, find out why.
How many people have held this job in the past five years?	To see if the position is a difficult one to succeed in.
How many people have been promoted from this position in the past five years?	To determine whether the job is a springboard to bigger and better things.
What would be your highest priority for me to accomplish if you hired me?	To get an idea about what your real priorities will be. Do global responsibilities translate into substantive tasks or something less?
How independent is this department?	To judge whether you will be able to get things done.
Why did you join the company? How long have you been here? Why do you stay?	To test your interviewer's enthusiasm for the company or reservations about it.
What kind of travel is associated with the job? Where would I be working most of the time? Tell me about the company's travel policies.	To avoid surprises about working conditions you might not be aware of unless you ask.
Will I be attending a training program? Where and for how long?	To find out both the opportunities and limitations in the staff training area.
Is there a formal job description? Can I see it?	To determine if what you are hearing matches what is on paper. Are they making a minor position sound too important? Or vice versa?
Tell me about the evaluation process at this company. When will my first review come, and how important is it?	To find out how the reward and advancement structure link to performance.

Don't ask things that you could have looked up in the annual report or a standard business reference. Don't put your interviewer on the spot. Orient your questions toward things that you need to know to make an intelligent career decision. Leave salary and benefits questions for the negotiating stage. Don't ask how you did in the interview! Keep your questions, attitude, and expectations positive.

DEALING WITH INTERVIEWERS

You don't want to make your preparation too obvious. There is something disconcerting about the overprepared candidate, so avoid giving that impression. Make sure your interviewer walks away with the feeling that he or she has communicated with the person you will be day to day on the job, not an actor who learned his or her lines. Let your knowledge of the company show as the interview unfolds—not all at once.

The same is true of asking your own questions. Wait until they fit. Don't fall into the coached-candidate trap of dropping an obviously planted question and awkwardly trying to make it mean something when it doesn't. You will have your chance to ask real questions in the course of your interview and at its conclusion.

TYPES OF INTERVIEWERS

You can expect to encounter two basic types of interviewers:

1. the personnel or human resources professional; and
2. the line manager, supervisor, or senior executive.

This division separates the people who do the work of the company: the managers, supervisors, and executives; and the personnel or human resources people who support them.

The personnel staff is most heavily involved in the screening stage of hiring. Their job is to select a basically qualified group of candidates from which the decision makers can hire. The line manager is the person you end up working for after the hiring is over. Personnel's continuing role includes employee benefits administration and maybe some training. Each of the two types of interviewers has an orientation you should be aware of.

When it comes to interviewing, expect managers as a group to be commonsense generalists—they will use fewer interviewing techniques, such as deliberately adding stress. Managers are more interested in getting to know you and determining whether you know your stuff, want to do the work required, and would be nice to work with.

Human resources people are more apt to use interviewing technique tricks. They read the journals, think more like psychologists, and, as a group, are more interested in sorting applicants in seemingly objective ways. They want to get the verifiable facts about you. Personnel interviewers apply the objective hiring criteria given to them by management and weed you out if you give them an obvious reason to. They also give you basic information about the company—everything from the corporate culture to employee benefits. In short, they save the line manager the time and trouble of doing the preliminaries. In smaller organizations the manager often performs some of the roles left to personnel in larger corporations.

With the distinction between the two kinds of interviewers in mind, you can see how their approaches will differ. Expect personnel to test your fit against formal job criteria. Expect managers to have a more hands-on approach to evaluating your suitability. Increasingly, personnel interviewers are trained to get beyond the defenses of the prepared candidate. In many companies, interviewing skills of human resources professionals are taught to managers and supervisors as well.

INTERVIEWERS' TECHNIQUES

Today no sooner does the candidate learn the tricks of the interviewer than the interviewer develops new ones. Articles in personnel journals and business magazines are now busy telling human resources managers how to train interviewers to get beyond the hype of the well-prepped candidate. Dan Moreau, in *Changing Times*, writes:

> Oh, for the good old days, when job interviews were job interviews, and you could whiz through one by volleying the stock questions with your glib, prepackaged answers. Today it's not so easy. Job interviewers have wised up. Now they're more apt to press a point—to take a line from your resume, for example, and ask you in depth about it. Why did you choose that college? What projects did you complete there that would make you a better candidate for the job we have?
> Looking good in your job interview today means preparing for the unexpected.

A number of managers are being prepared to take more than an impromptu approach to their role as interviewers. In an *Industry Week* article on hiring, James Braham quoted a TRW, Inc., director of management development who said "...we're trying to make sure that our managers know how to ask some follow-up questions, probe deeper into the subject area, and get away from that practiced answer—really get to know the candidate better. You look for how he deals with others, what are his communication skills, his motivation? Does he set goals? Have high energy? How does he solve problems?" Here are some techniques currently being used to get beyond your preparation for the standard interview questions and find out what you are really like.

NEGATIVE REFERENCE CHECK

Routine references and letters of recommendation are notoriously positive—otherwise you wouldn't provide them. At the most, they may damn with faint praise, and they rarely describe a truly negative incident or characteristic. To get around that, employers will sometimes ask, during the interview, for the names of several people whom you did not get along with very well. The practice was described in *INC.* magazine by consultant Phil Thomas:

> While most job applicants will say initially they can't think of anyone who didn't like them, persistence will almost always result in some names—names that the surprised applicant probably hasn't had time to screen mentally. Those negative references and the potential hire's explanations of the problems invariably give...a more balanced picture of the person's strengths and weaknesses.

Your best tactic as an applicant going into such a situation is to have several people in mind who were not your soul mates in previous work settings but whose respect you ended up commanding. Think of people with whom you had honest differences, never really won over, but who would respond when asked that you were a bright, fair-minded person who just happened to see things differently from the way they did.

NETWORK REFERENCE CHECK

Networking is a two-way street in hiring. While you can enhance your knowledge of the company and the interviewing process, so, too, can the company investigate you and verify your claims. Consultants interviewed in Braham's *Industry Week* article expressed the belief that people applying for professional positions have reputations within their industry. Personnel staff, managers, and executives can check you out on a quiet, personal level by contacting professional acquaintances and seeking candid opinions about you and your work. Consider the connections that might logically exist between your professional associates in your present and past positions and those who will want to know more about you at the new firm. Anticipate calls that might take place, and consider preparing people who are not among your formal references for the possibility of being contacted about your application for the new position. The less people are surprised, the better are your chances of getting favorable reviews on impromptu reference checks.

TWO-SIDED-COIN QUESTIONS

A smooth reference checker will put the person being queried at ease by asking mostly positive questions about you. Of course, even positive questions can probe things that are not apparent in the sometimes complimentary but revealing responses they bring out. An example might be, "Tell me the area in which Jill showed her greatest growth during the period she worked with you." In answering, the reference often doesn't think about the mirror side of that question, which is that he or she is also revealing your area of greatest weakness—the thing you had to work on. This is not bad—you overcame the problem—but it illustrates how a seemingly harmless question can have a hidden agenda.

BEHAVIORAL INTERVIEWING

Jim Kennedy, a San Francisco consultant quoted by James Braham in *Industry Week*, thinks that the hiring advantage has swung from the employer to the candidate. The reason is the current emphasis on preparing candidates to ace the standard interview. College placement officers, outplacement companies, executive recruitment firms, and self-help books have made a concerted effort to train candidates for their interviews. Companies have reacted by turning to interviewing techniques designed to do more than just hear what the candidate says about his or her job performance and training. Now they expect candidates to reveal *how* and *what* they did in concrete terms—less fluff, more verifiable substance. What you did and how you did it are what your interviewer wants to know to visualize your behavior on the job.

CONTINUUM QUESTIONS

One way interviewers draw you out is to give you a question that has no right or wrong answer—no boundaries—and see what you do with it. It is merely designed to "work you" and let the interviewer judge how well you do everything from "handling yourself" to fitting in with the company. You are also given the rope with which to hang yourself, if you are so inclined. The question might involve asking you what kind of relationship you prefer with your boss—highly structured or unstructured, for example. Either approach to answering it could be productive and "correct." What the interviewer wants to explore is your values, work ethic, and style—as well as your ability to deal with an ambiguous question.

A TO Z QUESTIONS

Consultant Kurt Einstein's A to Z method is described in Bruce Posner's *INC.* magazine article. It recommends getting you to open up by describing your three most sterling accomplishments in as much detail as possible. "What are the three professional highlights of your career so far? Tell me all about each one of them. What did you do? How did you do it? Why is it so important to you?" The approach puts the focus on you, the candidate, what you personally did and how you did it, instead of the accomplishments of your department, boss, or other third parties. It is a combination open-ended and follow-up question that is supposed to get you away from scripted responses and provide more in-depth information about yourself. The A to Z question is open enough to give you a chance to demonstrate what is important to you, what you can get enthusiastic about, and so on.

TARGETED SELECTION QUESTIONS

Kirsten Schabacker, writing in *Working Woman*, mentioned a Pittsburgh consulting firm that uses an interviewing technique called targeted selection designed to reveal how a candidate thinks and acts. Some questions illustrating the technique included

- "Tell me about a particularly successful presentation you made in your last job and why it was such a success. What about a not-so-successful one? What went wrong?"
- "Tell me about a project you worked on in which one of the team members was not really pulling his or her weight."

This technique is designed to put you on the spot for a specific issue and force a revealing response. It puts you into a situation of having to acknowledge that everything isn't perfect in your work experience and makes you tell how you handled the problems and were affected by them.

Handling Inappropriate Questions

There are some things you are protected from answering, and most interviewers are aware of that. Your religion; political beliefs; ancestry; national origin; birthplace and naturalization status of your parents, spouse, or children; native language or language spoken at home; age (except to say that you are over eighteen); ages of your children; marital status; maiden name; spouse's occupation; and number of dependents—these are among a long list of questions you should never be expected to answer. If an interviewer stumbles across one of them, you have several choices:

- Politely ask its relevancy for the position in question.

- Refuse to answer, and cite your rights protected by the Equal Employment Opportunity Commission, or

- Volunteer the information if you think it might be helpful and the interviewer seems to want to know.

It is a judgment call on your part. The whole issue of equal opportunity is discussed more fully in Chapter 8, "Interviewing and the Law." The area of sexual attraction can also bring about inappropriate lines of questioning, comments, and innuendos; Chapter 9 advises you on how to deal with that problem if it arises.

SUMMARY CHECKLIST: PREPARING FOR THE INTERVIEW

- Your preparations begin with an examination of the standard business references and proceed to sources unique to your region and industry.

- Your objectives in preparing for your interview are to secure the interview and do well during it.

- Your focus in preparing for your interview should include sources of information, the company and its people, what you want and have to offer, and the interview process and how you can influence it.

- Your sources of information include library and other business references, community organizations, regional and national publications, the Internet, and your network of friends and professional acquaintances.

- You need to sort out what you need to know about the company, why you want to know it, and where you can find the answers.

- Your interview can assume a variety of formats, and familiarity with each of them helps you prepare for and avoid surprises.

- Interviewers follow expected procedures, and knowing them can make you a more effective candidate.

- Interviewers ask certain kinds of questions, and anticipating them can help you answer effectively.

- You are expected to ask some questions of your own, and there are certain ones that both impress interviewers and help you understand the job.

- You can cause problems for yourself by appearing to be overly prepared.

- Interviewers are either personnel/human resources types or managers, and they have different approaches to interviewing.

- Interviewers have developed techniques designed to get beyond your prepared answers; you should know what they are and how to handle them.

3 APPEARING FOR THE INTERVIEW

Much of the impression you leave with your interviewer is subjective—it is the gut feeling he or she gets when you walk in the door. You can improve that impression by being at ease and free of distractions when you become the focus of attention. Some things that can help you do that include:

- dressing properly;
- being comfortable with your appearance;
- knowing exactly where you are going;
- knowing the procedures;
- being aware of whom to expect; and
- being aware of what to expect.

In this chapter you review the accepted way of doing everything from shaking hands to saying hello and good-bye. You learn the procedures for dealing with interviewers' names, judging the right time to arrive, sensing when to leave, and everything else that makes your entrance, presence, and exit smoothly executed events. When you do all of these things well, it leaves the focus on you and your positive attributes instead of on memorably awkward moments that could have been avoided.

Before you go on to the detailed suggestions about showing up for your appointment, review Figure 3 below and put what you are about to learn into context. Understand how your efforts to apply for the job, secure the interview, and research

GETTING THE INTERVIEW
- Finding a job
- Applying
- Networking
- Getting invited

PREPARING FOR THE INTERVIEW
- Researching the company
- Preparing personally
- Anticipating questions

APPEARING FOR THE INTERVIEW
- Reconnaissance
- Personal readiness
- Timing

You have done your research, have prepared yourself as best as you could, and now it's time to meet the interviewer. You are confident about your company knowledge and your own qualifications, and don't want an awkward arrival to detract from your positive image. You discreetly check out the interview site so there's no chance of getting lost or being late. You know what the appropriate interview dress is and wear it. Good grooming, manners, and knowledge of what to say and do complete your preparations for a relaxed, on-time arrival.

DURING THE INTERVIEW
- Names and personalities
- Style and substance
- Satisfying agendas

LEAVING THE INTERVIEW
- Reading your audience
- Positive expectations
- Last impression

EVALUATING YOUR INTERVIEW
- Substantive match
- Personal chemistry
- Judging your chances

FOLLOWING UP AFTER YOUR INTERVIEW
- Thank you's
- Additional information
- More networking

CONCLUDING THE INTERVIEW PROCESS
- The offer
- Negotiating
- Accepting

Figure 3. Appearing for the Interview

and otherwise prepare for it have advanced you to the point of appearing for the culmination of all that effort—the face-to-face job interview.

"Appearing for the Interview" covers the practical matters of getting to your interview session looking good, feeling good, and situated to do your best. It is the chance to make your pitch for a job you really want. You have enough on your mind without worrying about how to find the building, what the parking arrangements are like, and the location of the last unlocked rest room before you become identified as "the candidate." You don't want to be lost, late, inappropriately attired—or have your first words be "May I have the key to your rest room?"

This chapter is filled with practical, commonsense suggestions. Many of them are precautions you might have taken anyway. Others are things you may never have thought about. But before you decide that it sounds all *too* obvious, look at some true stories of what takes place at job interviews.

As the titles imply, the authors of these two articles were looking for the extreme cases and found them, but in doing so they make the point that there are codes of behavior for job interviews that you want to be sensitive to. After you see how far some people go in the wrong direction, learn this chapter's down-to-earth lessons about how you should behave.

According to an article titled "Foolish Interviews" in *USAir Magazine*, Accountemps surveyed two hundred executives, asking them to cite the most unusual things they ever saw or heard of happening during job interviews. Here are some highlights:

- She returned that afternoon asking if we could redo the entire interview.
- He said if I hired him, I'd soon learn to regret it.
- She wanted to borrow the fax to send out some personal letters.
- He brought in a mini tape recorder and said he always taped his job interviews.
- She took three cellular phone calls. Said she had a similar business on the side.
- He left his dry-cleaner tag on his jacket and said he wanted to show he was a clean individual.
- When asked about loyalty, he showed a tattoo of his girlfriend's name.
- The candidate was told to take his time answering, so he began writing down each of his answers before speaking.

In a similar article, which *Harper's Magazine* called "Unemployment Strategies," you find excerpts from a survey sponsored by Robert Haft International, a major recruiting firm. Vice presidents and personnel directors of a hundred large corporations were asked to describe their most unusual interviewing experiences. Here are several techniques you might want to reconsider if you planned to include them in your job interview:

- Applicant challenged the interviewer to an arm wrestle.
- Interviewee wore a Walkman, explaining that she could listen to the interviewer and the music at the same time.
- Candidate fell and broke a bone during the interview.
- Candidate announced she hadn't had lunch and proceeded to eat a hamburger and French fries in the interviewer's office.
- Applicant explained that her long-term career goal was to replace the interviewer.
- Candidate said he never finished high school but was kidnapped and kept in a closet in Mexico.
- Balding candidate excused himself and returned to the office a few minutes later wearing a hairpiece.
- Applicant said if he were hired, he would demonstrate his loyalty by having the corporate logo tattooed on his forearm.
- Applicant interrupted interview to phone his therapist for advice on how to answer specific interview questions.
- Candidate brought large dog to the interview.
- Applicant refused to sit down and insisted on being interviewed standing up.
- Candidate dozed off and started snoring during interview.

Amusing? Yes. All that unusual? Not really. I remember a colleague coming to lunch one day following a busy morning of interviewing candidates. He told of his surprise—and only later, amusement—when a candidate entered his office and sat down in the *interviewer's* chair! He conducted the interview from the *candidate's* chair, and none of us ever forgot the incident. The prospect was not hired, and all that any of us recall is the chair incident—it obliterated any other impact that candidate might have made on us. The message to you is that it is worth being aware of and respecting the seemingly obvious protocols as you appear for your job interview. You have a role to play, and if you get too far out of character, you lose.

Clothing and Grooming

It is only common sense to come to your interview well groomed and properly dressed. But that takes judgment and sometimes presumes knowledge that you might not have. While the general rules are known to most candidates, a surprising number of us miss a link or two in the chain of perfect social graces as we make our way to becoming reasonably sophisticated adults. It is worth reviewing the suggestions that follow and doing a bit of research on what is expected where you plan to interview.

Internet Tip

Illustrations of currently fashionable professional wear can be found on the Internet at catalog sites like http://www.landsend.com and retailers like http://www.menswearhouse.com. Check your favorites using keywords and a search engine.

PROPER DRESS

If you are a military officer interviewing for a command position, there is no doubt about what you will wear. There is a correct uniform designated for the season and the occasion. All you need to worry about is having it fit well and be clean, pressed, and complete with the proper embellishments. In many instances it is actually designated the "uniform of the day"—you can't go wrong.

The same is nearly true in most businesses. Each situation has its "uniform," and with some effort you can determine what it is and comply. In the jargon of college town clothiers, what you are trying to describe is an "interview suit." Graduating seniors, certainly from business and law schools, invest in one. It is a tradition, a necessity, and an expectation of the recruiters who will interview them.

In selecting your interview suit, find safety in the norm—your job interview is no time to stand out in either direction. Good-quality business clothing, clean and well fitted, is your goal. Respect the seasonal nature of certain items by avoiding inappropriately light-colored garments except in summer—and then only if they are accepted in the group in which you will be interviewing. A perfectly proper summer tan business suit might be totally out of place in certain corporate or government offices even on a humid, ninety-eight-degree Washington, D.C., day. The same goes for short-sleeve shirts, as illogical as that may sound.

If you can't find out by observation what your interviewer and his or her colleagues will likely be wearing, call and ask the secretary what the usual business dress is for the office. There is no need to identify yourself. Just say you are coming to town on a future business trip and wanted to inquire. You can't go wrong with a moderately conservative dark suit (dark blue or gray is better than brown) that meets the current lapel width and fabric standards (natural or a blend), solid white or light blue shirt (cotton or a blend, never polyester, never a dark color), and a businesslike tie of current vintage, color, and width. A suit is preferred to a sport coat or blazer—no "leisure suits," if you still happen to have one (yes, they do still appear at interviews).

For men, dark dress shoes would usually be better than loafers, although dress slip-ons giving the appearance of wingtips or other business standards would be fine in most settings. Dark socks are essential—preferably the same color or a darker shade than the pants. Never, ever white! Over the calf is the preferred length. A dark belt of reasonable width for the suit and color match for the shoes is good—no casual belts with dress suits, please, and no dominant, attention-getting buckles.

Leave your gold chains and turquoise ring or watchband at home—avoid any jewelry that would be distracting. Men's earrings are increasingly common, but not recommended; even the unadorned pierced male ear can raise eyebrows.

Women have much the same situation as men, except it isn't as easy to select a "standard" business uniform. This is truer today than it was a few years ago, when women were into the male business look. You want to appear as an attractively attired woman avoiding the extremes of fashion. It is perfectly acceptable that you look pretty and feminine. It might not be wise to emphasize sex appeal, although that is a matter of personal judgment and varies by situation. (Chapter 9, "Sex and the Interview," discusses this more fully.) For most women, a modest, well-fitting dress or suit would probably be fine. Slacks are not a good idea. Tasteful, interesting jewelry is fine, but choose things that will not be a distraction for your interviewer.

It is not necessary to buy a wardrobe item or accessory for the interview, unless you are in a rare situation where it would clearly benefit you. Here is an example of how you can handle even that inexpensively when necessary. Amy Bernstein noted in *U.S. News & World Report* that there are businesses that cater to the special needs of job interview candidates:

> In a tough job market like today's, no applicant wants to be caught without the proper corporate accoutrements. That's where the London Harness Co. of Boston comes in: For $38, yuppie-wannabes can rent a classic leather briefcase worth $950, which ought to impress a prospective employer. So far, only two or three customers have used the service. Maybe London Harness ought to expand to lease-a-power-tie.

GOOD GROOMING

The starting point is cleanliness. Above all else, be freshly bathed and have your hair recently cut, shampooed, and styled in some acceptable business fashion. Avoid the extremes, whether you are a man or a woman. If your hair is colored, have it done by a professional. On the job you will be representing the company to its clients, and you will be silently judged during the interview on the image you project. Do-it-yourself hair coloring, extreme haircuts, and overdone makeup all contribute to a silent selection-out process that can destroy what is otherwise a substantively good interview.

Use deodorant—unscented is fine, even preferred. Don't use heavy perfume, cologne, or aftershave. A touch of something is fine, especially on women. Men: when in doubt, opt for the clean, unscented image that doesn't raise the question of whether your interviewer likes what you are wearing—or, for that matter, whether she or he thinks you should be wearing it. If you insist on splashing the aftershave at the last opportunity (and I recommend against it), wash your hands! The last thing you need is for the interviewer with whom you have just shaken hands to sit there smelling your overpowering scent on his or her own hand throughout the interview.

Facial hair for men is usually a negative. If you are coming for an interview in the traditional business world, leave the full-face beard behind. A reasonable-size and well-kept mustache may be acceptable, although in some cities certain styles send a message you may not intend. When in doubt, come clean-shaven for a serious job interview. If it is important to you, check the situation out beforehand by asking someone not in your interviewing chain if beards are not unusual in the organization.

Visible body hair on women can be distracting in our culture. Without arguing the merits, I recommend adhering to the usual expectations: shaved underarms, legs, and appropriately removed noticeable facial hair.

DO'S AND DON'TS OF CLOTHING AND GROOMING	
Do	**Don't**
Select moderately conservative business wear for your interview—wear the "uniform."	Try to make a fashion statement or express your individualism.

(cont'd)

Do	Don't
Choose blue, charcoal or gray, solid or modest pinstripe (women have more flexibility, but these are always correct).	Choose black, brown, or another color.
Wear a long-sleeve solid (or very muted pinstripe) white or light blue shirt (women have more flexibility but can't go wrong with these).	Wear dark shirts, bold colors or patterns, or short sleeves.
Dress with the season and situation in mind. Wear a dark business dress in the summer if that is the accepted style.	Wear summer colors in other seasons.
Wear dress shoes—tie or slip-on (men).	Wear "comfort sole" dress shoes.
Coordinate shoes and belts—both should be leather, a deep brown or black (women are safe adding navy, burgundy, or even red). For women, choose moderate heels or flats.	Wear casual accessories with dress clothes or showy belt buckles.
Men: wear over-the-calf socks as dark or darker than your suit. Women: wear conservative skin-tone hosiery.	Men: wear white socks or inappropriate lengths (crew or midcalf) or colors (especially light ones). Women: wear highly styled, patterned, black, white, or colored hosiery.
Wear natural or blended fabrics—modern wools are best.	Wear polyester fabrics.
Wear a suit or business dress.	Wear a sport coat or pantsuit.
Men: wear a reasonably conservative, good-quality, contemporary-style tie. Women: optional with some business fashions—same standard if a scarf is selected.	Wear a bow or a too wide/narrow light or patterned tie or scarf.

(cont'd)

Do	Don't
Wear modest jewelry and accessories—analog watch and leather band.	Wear garish, dominant, or ostentatious jewelry and accessories—skin diver watches or fraternal/political pins.
Let your natural attractiveness show modestly.	Make your physical attractiveness a feature of your presentation.
Dress for the position you want.	Dress for the position you have.
Dress to the accepted standard of your industry—conservative business dress is right for most but not all situations. Inquire if in doubt.	Show your individuality by expressing a personal standard at interview time. Wear regional fashions such as western wear—even of the finest quality—unless you are where it will be unquestionably accepted.
Carry a plain brown or burgundy leather briefcase (blue or black may also be okay for women with the right outfit).	Carry a "stand-out" briefcase full of embellishments or a soft-sided fabric model with your initials monogrammed on it. Juggle both purse and briefcase (use a small clutch in the briefcase instead).
Carry only what you need.	Carry an overcoat, a newspaper, book, or other accessories that are not essential. Stuff your pockets with bulging, unessential things.
Choose a light scent or unscented grooming and beauty products for your interview.	Wear something that is bound to get attention—it might be the thing that is most memorable about you.
Emphasize cleanliness in preparing yourself for the interview—body, hair, and clothes.	Present an unkempt appearance or show any signs of poor hygiene.
Brush your teeth. Visit your dentist for a professional cleaning if it has been a while.	Eat offending foods before the interview.

(cont'd)

Do	Don't
Men: appear clean-shaven—although a well-kept mustache will usually be okay.	Appear with a beard unless you have prior knowledge that it will be well received.
Present the appearance of a non-smoker.	Show the telltale signs of being a smoker—stained fingers and teeth, the smell of stale smoke on your clothes and papers, smoking materials in your briefcase or pockets.

Familiarizing Yourself with the Interview Site

For a comfortable arrival, know where you are going and what conditions to expect when you get there. You can remove this form of anxiety by checking out the site ahead of time. Locally you do that by deliberately going across town for a dry run one afternoon. If you are traveling to a distant city, you might find it necessary to arrive the evening before. This is not always necessary if you know the setting from previous business trips. You may also have a totally straightforward situation that leaves no room for doubt. However, you will arrive more relaxed if you inquire about the exact location, parking arrangements, and special considerations of which you should be aware—such as highway construction that may make you late, for example.

RECONNAISSANCE

If you live in the interview city or can arrive at an out-of-town site early, go to the building where your interview will be held and satisfy yourself on these matters:

- If you're driving, is parking available, or is it available only to people working in the building? If so, ask your interviewer to arrange with the garage to expect you or to suggest an alternative.

- Is the traffic pattern at the time you will arrive the same as when you checked the site? Are some streets one-way during rush hour? etc.

- Is public transportation convenient if you don't plan to drive?

- Are there any special building security arrangements? Have you been listed as an expected guest for the day of your interview?

- Is the office easy to locate, or will special instructions be necessary?
- What time do the facilities you plan to use open and close if you will arrive early and/or stay late?

These matters are not always taken care of by your host. If the information isn't volunteered by the time your interview draws near, find out for yourself and ask for assistance.

Internet Tip

Internet map sites will help you find your way to an interview. Enter the employer's address and get back a detailed map and driving instructions—but remember to check it for real-world accuracy. Suggested sites include Mapquest.com or the map feature on the Yahoo.com. You can also enter the keyword "maps" and locate others.

In addition to putting your mind at ease about these matters, your comfortable arrival gives you time to learn more about the job and the company. A chat with the doorman could reveal that the company will be in its new suburban headquarters this time next year. Or small talk with the parking lot attendant tells you about a commuter bus that leaves the shopping center near your apartment to that suburban complex every weekday morning.

If your plans include an overnight stay before your interview, ask if your hotel room is quiet. I once arrived for a critical business meeting in Cleveland and retired for the evening early in a nice hotel room only to be awakened at midnight by workmen using jackhammers to tear down a massive parking garage across the street. This is not the sort of thing reservations clerks volunteer, but they will usually admit it if you ask. Don't go into your interview tired and aggravated when problems like these can be avoided.

PIT STOPS AND PRIMPING

You can't expect to arrive for the interview and discreetly duck into the restroom. It is increasingly common to find them locked. The answer, short of beginning your visit with an awkward request for the bathroom key, is for you to learn ahead of time where a public restroom is available. That kind of information can be picked up during your preliminary walk-through.

You should not overlook the practical side of interviewing—restrooms and otherwise. Your best-laid plans for what to say and how to say it in the interview session can be rendered less effective by being personally uncomfortable. Foresight can eliminate the problem entirely, leaving the interview itself as the focus of your valuable energies and attention.

Interviewing Procedures

There are things that you just need to do "right" when it comes to interviewing. They are not written in stone and there are exceptions, but you should have a sense of what will be well received and what will be offensive. You don't want to detract from your otherwise favorable impression at the interview by doing the little things wrong. Here are some examples.

TIMING YOUR ARRIVAL

You don't want to be late for your interview, but neither do you want to be uncomfortably early—for you or your host. If you arrive more than ten minutes ahead of schedule, plan to kill time inconspicuously somewhere besides the reception area of your interviewer. The ideal situation is to walk in about five minutes early. You run the risk of awkwardly encountering the person interviewing before you if you are too far ahead of schedule. That could prove embarrassing for everyone concerned in certain situations. Avoid the problem by being only slightly early.

WHAT TO BRING AND WHAT TO LEAVE AT HOME

In the interview "bloopers" that introduced this section, you learned not to bring your lunch, a Walkman, or a large dog. It is almost as bad to come with your spouse and children or anyone else whose presence is a distraction. If your interview is extended or you are taken to lunch, you then have an added problem.

On the practical side, bring a briefcase or folio with you with a copy of your resume, a completed application if you have one, a list of your references (possibly several letters of reference), and a few samples of your work if you need to exhibit it. It is a good idea to have a small pad on which to take notes if that becomes appropriate during your interview. You should also have the telephone numbers of your contacts in case you are unexpectedly delayed. A list of questions you would like to have answered is also an appropriate thing to have readily available. Don't forget your directions for finding the interview site, and a map if you need one.

HANDSHAKES AND GREETINGS

You wouldn't think that saying hello or shaking hands would present a problem, and usually they don't. However, done memorably wrong, they can mark you as an inept candidate and detract from an otherwise good impression.

Your handshake should be extended only in response to one offered by your interviewer. Never initiate it. Make your grip pleasantly firm—neither crushing nor limp. If you in fact have "sweaty palms," inconspicuously dry them before coming into the greeting situation—fold your handkerchief and replace it in your pocket, for example, and discreetly dry your handshaking palm in the process. Reach inside your briefcase and find a freshly folded cloth handkerchief there that will accomplish the same thing. It would be an unusual business interview that began with a "high-five," so resist the urge to greet even a long-lost friend with other than the traditional handshake until the two of you are in a less formal situation.

When greetings are made, your host or hostess should be allowed to take the initiative. If you are sure you know names, use them. When in doubt, pause until everyone's identity is made known. The use of first names is inappropriate unless you are invited to do so by the interviewer; even then, switch back to more formal address if someone else joins the interview. If you are in a panel interview and know only some of the people well, use formal address for everyone until a more relaxed atmosphere has been introduced. While you will almost certainly be met and escorted during the course of your interviews, if you find yourself directed to a series of offices, rely on the secretary at each location to introduce you. If you end up truly on your own, just do the natural, polite thing and say: "Ms. Jones? My name is John Wilson, and I was asked to talk with you about the accounting vacancy. I am a candidate for the position." She should take it from there; follow her lead.

You need to handle the question of personal titles carefully. Mr. and Ms. are the safest these days—Mrs. is fine if you are certain of its correctness. If a genderless functional title makes for a comfortable greeting—such as the dean of a college—use it: "Good morning, Dean Smith, it is a pleasure to meet you." Dr. is fine if you are sure that the title is correct, but don't put a person into the awkward position of having to explain that he doesn't have a doctorate. In terms of your own title, modesty is best. "Good afternoon, I'm Don Jackson" is usually better than "Good afternoon, I'm Dr. Jackson," unless you are a medical doctor. Academic doctoral degrees are often best understated. Outside the military, that rule is doubly true for rank—you should be "Colonel" Smith to your military associates only, not to your civilian colleagues, unless it is a situation that clearly warrants using the title.

The best use of titles—academic, military, and otherwise—is to have other people "discover" you have them; never announce them yourself. In job interviews this can have practical implications for you. For example, your interviewer may be a very accomplished person with no formal titles. While she or he would not likely say so, chances are it would be appreciated if you don't emphasize them either. The fact that you have them speaks for itself via your credentials; soft-pedal the issue in person and you will appear the more gracious for doing so.

SEATING

The natural and correct approach is to let your interviewer show you where to sit. The same is true of timing your seating—follow the lead of your interviewer, who will indicate that you should be seated. If none of this materializes, just wait the interviewer out and take the most obviously correct chair after she or he has been seated. When someone else enters the room, stand and be prepared to shift chairs to accommodate the individual if he or she stays.

PHYSICAL CONDITION

You relate better to your interviewer if you feel and look well. One of the most telling things about first impressions is the image of your overall condition that you telegraph by your appearance. Not just the suit and haircut, but also the clarity of your eyes, the erectness of your posture, the spring in your step, your engaging smile. Taken together, things like these tell the interviewers important things. Here are a few tips on how you can make that subjective impression a positive one.

- *Rest*—You want to look rested. It shows when you are worn out. Obvious fatigue can be taken as a sign of a lifestyle and personal habits that might detract from your ability to work effectively. Get a good night's sleep each night for a week before interviewing. Avoid emotional aggravation—the week of the interview is not a good time to leave your spouse or bring on other weighty problems. Such things show on your face. You want to present your interviewer with the peaceful, rested look of someone whose life is in good order.

- *Exercise*—A tiring workout just before the interview is a bad idea. An ongoing exercise program that gets you in shape by the time of the interview is a good one. If your career move lends itself to long-range planning and exercise is not yet part of your routine, add it to your lifestyle six months before you get serious about the job search. You will look better, feel better about yourself, and have something in common with your interviewer, who is apt to be doing the same thing these days. In a dynamic office of the 1990s you are probably the exception if you are not into some kind of fitness routine. The topic may very well come up in the course of your interview, and you will fit the office culture more comfortably if you have the established habit. Today, showing a personal concern for one's own health and fitness is the norm. You can do that with an individual training program that requires no particular athletic orientation, personal expense, or sacrifice of time; extended lunch hours often accommodate the office exerciser. Company benefits and even compensation packages are increasingly geared to your willingness to stay fit. It can have a favorable impact at interview time as well.

- *Relaxation*—You want to strike a businesslike balance between being hyperkinetic and too laid back. The two preceding topics, on rest and exercise, are an integral part of relaxation. The third component is a personal attitude toward your life and work. What you want to convey at your interview—not with expository statements in most cases, but by example—is that you are a high-energy performer who knows how to relax. The workaholic image is passé—you are still expected to go the extra mile, but with a degree of grace that leaves you looking and feeling good. Appearing appropriately relaxed at your interview is your best way to telegraph this favorable impression. You do it by pulling together all the suggestions that have been made so far—be prepared for the interview, dress right, know where you are to be and arrive on time, be rested and fit. With those things done, the image you want to convey will come through naturally, and you will be ahead of the game because your competition can't fake it or put it together on short notice.

THINGS TO AVOID

Don't smoke, chew gum, make nervous gestures, or fail to respect people's personal space (getting too close when you speak, etc.). Articles and books can advise you about the power of body language and eye contact, but it all boils down to your exhibiting reasonable, normal behavior. While a more detailed discussion of body language follows under "Interview Psychology" in Chapter 4, here are some things to keep in mind:

Most interviewers will be uncomfortable with you if you don't look them in the eye. They will probably be just as uncomfortable if all you *do* is look them in the eye! Relax and interact as comfortably and naturally as you can, looking at the interviewer most of the time but casting your gaze elsewhere at intervals. Do not lean awkwardly forward for the whole interview. Again, relax, and sit as you would normally in a business conversation. Grow animated when the situation calls for it; sit back and be pensive when that is appropriate. Come across as a normal human being and not an actor at an audition.

You should be evaluating those who interview you on these same criteria. If an interviewer's desk has an ashtray overflowing with cigarette butts, you are in the wrong place if you are a nonsmoker. An interviewer whose gaze never leaves you could be an awkward supervisor in the workaday world. With the rare exception of "stress" interviews that should end with a return to normal interviewer behavior after you've been "tested," interviews should be an accurate window on the work environment. If anything, people are on better behavior during interviews, so take that into account in your follow-up evaluation of the session.

Whom and What to Expect

Internet Tip

Find the company's Web page by entering its name in a search engine or by using a site especially designed to locate company Web pages:
http://pic2.infospace.com/_1_244791928_info.jbank/bizweb.htm.
Also try the keywords "all in one" in a search engine to locate a site that includes specialized search engines for locating high-tech companies, etc.

If you have not been given a list of people you can expect to see in the course of your interview, make your own list. This can reduce your anxiety level. Everything you can put in the "expected to happen" column takes something off the list of possible surprises—and it really doesn't matter if they actually occur or not. For example, if the chairman of the board stops by for an urgent word with your interviewer and you had considered the possibility of meeting him, you take it comfortably in stride when he gives you a polite handshake. Had you not even considered the possibility, your response might have been more awkward.

Some people benefit from laying out their whole interview day complete with a cast of characters that includes everyone from the parking lot attendant to the boss's boss. You can plan to remember the receptionist's name—and do it because it is a deliberate, planned event. Remember that the receptionist, while not one of your raters, can be a positive influence with those who are. Also, how you treat support staff can influence your hiring. Your behavior toward other people may be scrutinized by your interviewer. Don't even slight the parking garage attendant—he or she just may have an informal vote before the day ends, when your interviewer heads off into the evening rush hour.

SUMMARY CHECKLIST: APPEARING FOR THE INTERVIEW

- To make your interview appearance effective, dress properly, be well groomed, know where you are going, handle the social protocols graciously, and be aware of whom and what to expect.

- Be aware of legendary job candidate "bloopers," avoid them yourself, and steer clear of less obvious but potentially disastrous missteps of your own.

- You should plan to dress in normal business attire; when in doubt, wear your "interview suit."

- Your grooming should emphasize cleanliness, a lack of extremes in scents and accessories, and modest good taste.

- You should make a familiarization visit to your interview site if practical and you haven't been there before.

- You should attend to your personal comfort and primping before arriving at the interviewer's office.

- You should arrive a few minutes ahead of time, never late or more than ten minutes early.

- Bring something on which to take notes, a copy of your resume, application, and references—and little else (no companions).

- Follow your interviewer's lead on handshakes and greetings, never initiating them yourself.

- Use your personal titles modestly and other people's professional titles correctly—avoiding first names unless their use is clearly indicated by your interviewer.

- Follow your interviewer's lead and gestures in seating.

- Appear for your interview rested, relaxed, and physically fit—qualities that speak volumes for your character and potential.

- Make a list of probable characters for your interview day and treat them all with interest and respect—not just your interviewer and his or her superiors.

- Use your interview to evaluate the corporate culture and decide whether you want to be part of it—smoking or nonsmoking, relaxed or formal, philosophically compatible with your values, etc.

4

DURING THE INTERVIEW

You now know about the preliminaries. You have located the job, successfully applied for it, researched the situation thoroughly, secured an interview appointment, and even studied the art of making an effective appearance. It is time to learn how to conduct yourself during the interview.

Your role at this point is to command the respect of the interviewer with your qualifications, honesty, motivation, and knowledge of the working situation. Your interviewer subtly tests each of these factors and at least informally evaluates your personality. And since an interview is only partly objective, you want:

- to be interesting and likable—an employer rarely hires anyone she or he doesn't first "like";

- to be your own strongest advocate, in a tactful and courteous way;

- to control a large part of the interview by injecting your own points as you answer the interviewer's questions and ask some of your own;

- to use your voice and personal style to impress the interviewer in ways that were not possible on paper; and

- to avoid leaving intangible negative impressions.

These are subjective aspects of the interview—things that don't necessarily fit on checklists but that have a way of registering with the interviewer and influencing his or her final judgment.

You are ready to use the information found during your research on the com-

GETTING THE INTERVIEW
- Finding a job
- Applying
- Networking
- Getting invited

PREPARING FOR THE INTERVIEW
- Researching the company
- Preparing personally
- Anticipating questions

APPEARING FOR THE INTERVIEW
- Reconnaissance
- Personal readiness
- Timing

DURING THE INTERVIEW
- Names and personalities
- Style and substance
- Satisfying agendas

LEAVING THE INTERVIEW
- Reading your audience
- Positive expectations
- Last impression

EVALUATING YOUR INTERVIEW
- Substantive match
- Personal chemistry
- Judging your chances

FOLLOWING UP AFTER
YOUR INTERVIEW
- Thank you's
- Additional information
- More networking

CONCLUDING THE
INTERVIEW PROCESS
- The offer
- Negotiating
- Accepting

You are facing the interviewer and are engaged in an exchange that will leave a personal impression of your qualifications and desirability for the job. It is the interviewer's task to verify your credentials and clarify points—with an interest in both the substance and style of your responses. This is where you show knowledge, display judgment, assert values, demonstrate restraint, and exude charm. You and the interviewer estimate how well you might fit into the organization as well as how you'd actually perform the tasks involved. Information on paper and voices on telephones become real people interacting and subtly judging capability, likability, and promise.

Figure 4. During the Interview.

pany, the position, and the people interviewing you. You already know about the different kinds of interviews that you might encounter, the questions you can expect to be asked, and the answers you might give from reading about them in Chapter 2. Now you are going to concentrate on dealing with the person asking them—the practical, applied psychology of the interviewer interacting with you the job candidate. Specifically, you will see how to:

- project your personal qualities during the interview;
- understand the reasons for background checks;
- use your research from the preparations stage;
- deal with the interviewer's questions;
- understand basic job interview psychology; and
- communicate technological awareness.

Figure 4 shows where these steps fit into the total job-hunting and interview cycle. Examine it before you go, then learn how you can perform at your best during the interview.

Projecting Personal Qualities

It is time for you to come off the resume sheet and become flesh and blood. You are about to get your chance to fill in the blanks that remain for the people who already like what they see on paper but need confirmation. They want to be assured that you are someone with whom they would like to share their working hours. You have to satisfy their concerns in the total communication experience that is the face-to-face job interview.

BACKGROUND CHECKS

You succeed in a job interview by establishing your credibility. It is one of the first things you do, and it becomes the baseline from which all of your other claims are judged. A lot of the interviewer's assessment of your honesty is a gut feeling, but the measures are becoming increasingly objective. You can expect to encounter varying degrees of "resume analysis." A conscientious interviewer will look for and then probe any inconsistencies in your resume and personal comments.

As you learned in resume writing, you have to account for all time periods. Your dates of schooling and employment should connect logically, or you need to explain the lapses. Breaks in employment can be as innocent as student travel before beginning a career or as serious as a prison term. You have to assume that your job application will be formally investigated.

In the 1980s resume checking became a growth industry. Companies such as Credential Check in Michigan reported 25 percent annual growth; Fidelifacts in New York jumped 75 percent between 1984 and 1987, according to *Fortune*. One reason for this growth is the liability employers can incur if you misrepresent yourself before they hire you, and you do something wrong after they hire you. Avis Rent-A-Car was sued for not checking the jail record of an employee who committed a crime while working for the company. Here is what one large background checking firm listed as the most common lies by job applicants. In checking 100 resumes for a high-tech manufacturer, they found the following discrepancies:

- Wrong dates of employment—41
- Wrong dates of study—26
- Wrong size of previous salary—13
- Nonexistent employer—11
- Wrong grade point average—7

According to *INC.* magazine, there's a 30 percent chance that a resume will be wrong and a 3 percent chance that an applicant will fail to disclose a criminal record. The best way for companies to prevent such misrepresentations is to ask the right questions in writing and have you sign the application—with notification that it will be verified. When that is done, says Barry Bergman, president of the security firm interviewed by *INC.*, it "...makes it less likely that a degree in political science will become an engineering degree, or that three months at a previous job will become three years."

Margaret Mannix, writing in *U.S. News & World Report*, said that a 1991 study by Northwestern University found that 46 percent of the 320 companies surveyed don't request a transcript when hiring a new college graduate, 56 percent don't check faculty references, 37 percent never speak with personal references, 21 percent fail to verify the degree, and 18 percent don't check past employment. Looking at the other side of those statistics, it is apparent that you still stand an excellent chance of being found out if you are dishonest. There is a lot of checking going on, and you should come to your interview comfortable with the fact that your resume and comments will stand the test of verification if it comes.

The way you phrase your responses can affect the way an interviewer judges your honesty. According to Brian Dumaine, writing in *Fortune*, employers are weary of sweeping statements like "I was in charge of" or "I created"—these are often signs that the candidate is exaggerating. You should approach your interview with an unembellished, positive, objective version of what you have done and what you expect to be able to do for the employer. With every claim made you should be ready to offer a reference or data that will vouch for your veracity. There is no way for you to anticipate what the interviewer already knows about you; it is not worth stretching the truth and risking failure on the grounds of dishonesty or exaggeration. None of which is to say that you should accentuate the negative or turn your interview into a confessional; act in your own best interests, but do it honestly.

MAKING YOUR POINTS

Make the interview a platform for presenting your own case for being hired. While the interview takes place at the invitation of the hiring company whose employee is conducting the session, you are still half the show, and communication is a two-way street. You certainly shouldn't appear arrogant, but you should show confidence. You have two direct ways to communicate at the interview:

1. *Answering questions*—lets you modify the interviewer's approach and enables you to stress your own agenda. Anyone who has ever watched a politician respond to an interviewer's questions knows that the answers don't have to be limited to the questions. While you should not make exaggerated use of the technique, there is room for you to maneuver. Rehearse your answers if some of the easy-to-anticipate questions come your way. Case History 7 illustrates this technique.

2. *Asking questions*—presents you with an opportunity to focus the interview in your favor. By asking the right questions you can do more than gather information; you can also make your own case and create "readiness" in your interviewer's mind for accepting your point of view. Your well-chosen questions can set the mood or shift the emphasis of the interview. You should anticipate this and have several questions prepared. Case History 8 illustrates this technique.

MAINTAINING A POSITIVE ATTITUDE

Bring enthusiasm and energy to your interview. Don't dread the occasion and come across as though you would rather be anywhere else. That is exactly how some candidates hurt their prospects.

Enthusiasm is something you can generate and control. It is a matter of personal attitude. You are the one who sends the internal messages that make you feel

Case History 7—Situation

CONTROLLING THE INTERVIEW WITH YOUR ANSWERS

Background

Nick Clayton is a publicist at a large trade press who is seeking the director of publicity position with a small, independent book publisher. ❶ He knows that his interviewer will probably inquire why he wants to step off the career ladder at a major organization to join a small one. He plans to use every occasion he can during the interview to communicate his intention to make a purposeful lateral move. ❷ One way to do that is by expanding his answers to promote his own agenda—establishing that he has a sound rationale for making the move.

Situation

❸ Nick takes his place in the interviewer's office, exchanges pleasantries, and begins to deal with questions. "Tell me what kind of clients you've been handling at Hilton Press," the interviewer asks. He responds, "I've been arranging promotional tours for nonfiction authors for the past three years. ❹ As I understand it, about 85 percent of your production is nonfiction. ❺ I'd love to take a highly personalized package to the media contacts I've had to work with all this time on a mass-production basis—what a difference it would make!"

❻ "Where have you established contacts, Nick?" the interviewer asks. ❼ "Most of the major market talk-radio producers are professional acquaintances, and the top half-dozen or so national TV talk shows. ❽ I think they'd really light up if they had a look at your stuff—even the backlist titles are refreshingly different," he answers. "So you think you'll still be listened to when you're representing us?" the interviewer inquires. ❾ "You bet I do! What I can do for you is get my foot into doors I've already entered. Once inside, I will have the chance to do what I've always wanted to do—promote some things I feel strongly about and not just the next project on my calendar!"

Conclusion

So in the routine discourse of his interview, Nick explains again and again his heartfelt ❿ answer to the hiring firm's biggest question, "Why does this guy want to work for us?"

Case History 7—Analysis

CONTROLLING THE INTERVIEW WITH YOUR ANSWERS

General Strategy

Nick has the challenge of explaining why he wants to make a lateral move from a fast-track career in a large organization to a small one. He has already said he wants to; he is now going to demonstrate it by weaving the rationale into a number of his interview responses. That will show the interviewer that Nick knows what he is doing.

Specific Points

❶ You often sense issues that call for elaboration.

❷ You have the floor when answering questions and, with some good judgment, can stretch most answers to address your own agenda.

❸ Let your interviewer set the pace of the interview, but be ready to interject your points in addition to what is specifically asked.

❹ After answering the question, Nick established linkage between his past and the organization's present missions.

❺ In the same conversation he made clear his view of how his work would be more rewarding in the new situation.

❻ The interviewer asks another limited, direct question.

❼ Nick proceeds to answer the direct question objectively.

❽ Without yielding the initiative to the interviewer, Nick proceeds to explain why his past experience and new setting will make for a profitable marriage.

❾ Reading the "buy signal" indicating that the interviewer is hearing his message, Nick comes right out with his prime motivation for the change from big to small company roles.

❿ Let your answers address what you understand to be the real concerns, not just the formally worded questions. Do it by expanding your answers.

Case History 8—Situation

CONTROLLING THE INTERVIEW WITH YOUR QUESTIONS

Background

Rene Fitzgerald is an operating room nurse who has not been working for several years and is ❶ interested in returning part time. She once suffered from "burnout" and wants to be certain that the working environment at the hospital suits her ❷ lifestyle, which now calls for a high degree of independence and an ability to leave the job at the hospital door.

Situation

Rene's talents are very much in demand, so she has the luxury of shopping for the right situation. ❸ A nurse placement agency arranges an appointment for her with the director of nursing at Fern Memorial Hospital. She is given an opportunity to ❹ introduce herself and say why she is interested in working as an operating room nurse at Fern. While she takes the occasion ❺ to voice her concern with limiting stress, it is the ❻ questions she asks later that clearly indicate her agenda. The director ends the session with the customary "Thank you for answering my questions. ❼ Now are there any that I might answer for you?" Rene has ❽ laid the groundwork, so it is not a surprise when she asks: ❾ "Do you consistently have enough staff to let me work three days a week, not making me feel guilty when I say no to additional hours? What happens if I want to accompany my husband on a business trip and I give you several weeks' notice that I'll need a replacement on a certain day? Do you have operating room nurses who have worked part time and stayed in that capacity for a number of years? Could you suggest a few I might talk with about working conditions? I have to limit the intensity of my involvement. Talk with my references and verify what I can do for you, and why I have to do it this way."

Conclusion

Rene has special needs of her own. She communicates them with questions whose relevance was made clear earlier in the interview. ❿ In doing so she steers clear of mismatched expectations and gets the type of working situation she can sustain successfully.

Case History 8—Analysis

CONTROLLING THE INTERVIEW WITH YOUR QUESTIONS

General Strategy

Rene is in a position to be frank but does not want to be offensive or appear to be indifferent to the needs of her potential employer. She is using her interview as an occasion not only to respond to the employer's questions but also to ask important ones of her own. She does this with sensitivity by putting her questions into the context of her special needs and providing references to substantiate her unique circumstances.

Specific Points

❶ When you are in a high-demand field, you stand a better chance of customizing your working situation.

❷ You have reasons to limit your professional activity and need to say so.

❸ Your agency prescreens the situation and establishes the fact that the employer has an interest in talking with you even with limitations.

❹ When interviews begin with a personal introduction, this can be an opportunity to begin sketching the parameters of your special needs.

❺ In this instance, she mentions the need for limiting stress in her work.

❻ You get the opportunity to go beyond generalities by asking well-thought-out questions that address your specific needs.

❼ While you can ask periodic questions during the interview, generally your opportunity comes by invitation at the end.

❽ It helps to have set the tone, especially if your questions are limiting.

❾ Then in a series of targeted questions, you explore your concerns with the interviewer.

❿ The objective of asking questions is to get a realistic job picture.

a certain way—"self-talk" is a term sometimes used to describe the process of initiating your own moods and feelings. No one is proposing that you adopt an unrealistic long-range view of your life; if you have problems, get to work on solving them. But for something as limited in time as a job interview, which is rich in potential for helping you solve other problems, it is worth talking yourself into an enthusiastic position instead of accepting the negative one. You can stop the internal process that repeats the negative message and dampens your enthusiasm. Replace it with a positive one that will sustain you through the interview. You will be amazed at the difference in how you feel, act, and appear to other people.

There is nothing mysterious about the power of a positive attitude. Interviewers are attracted to positive candidates who radiate that they look forward to the challenge of the new job and are sure they can make a contribution. Along with a capable employee, they are looking for a fresh attitude that will contribute to the overall mood of the company—a "can do" attitude that might be infectious. In addition to your fine qualifications, that is what they want to see in you, and you can deliver it if you try.

TRANSFERRING YOUR ENTHUSIASM

Your enthusiasm can transfer to the interviewer as well. It is a quality you can bring with you to an interview that might otherwise have remained uninspired. It is your own very personal touch—the way you introduce a favorable measure of yourself that no one else can duplicate. You personalize your interview and become memorable in a way that no competing candidate can exactly match—you become unique in the interviewer's eyes, and that can be quite valuable at selection time, when the choice comes down to one among many who are technically qualified.

SELLING YOURSELF AS LIKABLE

Put yourself in the interviewer's position. You are both there for a business purpose, but any meeting of two people is also a social transaction. Literally everyone wants to be liked, including your interviewer. The easier you make it for her or him to feel liked, the more highly she or he will regard you as a candidate. You never escape the stratification of the interview where you each have separate roles, but neither do you get away from the human interaction that weighs so heavily in the final subjective act of one person selecting or rejecting another one.

Like all techniques in interviewing, you can get into trouble by awkwardly applying the likability approach. Don't try to make the interviewer your buddy. Actress Julia Roberts is quoted in *Playboy* magazine as saying that one of the best pieces of advice she received from her brother, actor Eric Roberts, was: "You have to remember that this is show *business,* not show *friendship."* Keep the businesslike air and the appropriate professional distance. But with those boundaries in place, let the likability factor come into play between the two of you. If the situation lends itself, find a common interest and share a properly limited appreciation of it. Look for the things about which you can honestly share some enthusiasm.

Attitude is very important. If you expect to like someone, you probably will. Go into your interview expecting to find a person there ready to interview you who has your best interests in mind—someone you can have good feelings about and with whom you will relate easily.

CONVEYING PERSONAL STYLE

Common courtesy is expected; it is something that can win you points with the interviewer and support staff. Say some genuine "thank you's" for the nice things that everyone along the way has done for you. Be tactful and self-effacing when it comes to potentially embarrassing statements or incidents. Take them in stride, and seize the opportunity to give your hosts a comfortable way out if they have caused an awkward moment. Your courtesy stands an excellent chance of being both appreciated and remembered—it is the kind of quality they would appreciate seeing in a colleague. Look for opportunities to *demonstrate* what you are like during the interview.

ADAPTING TO YOUR INTERVIEWER

Part of making your interview a success is your ability to complement the style and energy level of your interviewer. Pace yourself to the interviewer—if he or she is "laid back" and casual, be ready to accommodate that style with more informal responses than you might normally give. However, avoid the trap of joining the informal interviewer in a personal style that is so relaxed as to make you appear indifferent or disrespectful. What is normal behavior for the interviewer may not be suitable for you. Look for straightforward invitations to informality before fully joining in.

DRINKING AND SMOKING

If you have a meal with your interviewer, be cautious about too much relaxed familiarity. Order something simple that you can easily eat while carrying on a business conversation. You can decline the second drink or skip alcohol entirely. It is no longer awkward to decline a cocktail; most people are now perfectly comfortable ordering a nonalcoholic drink. While this is an opportunity to establish that you drink socially (if indeed you do), you do not have to provide excuses for not drinking.

However, for recovering alcoholics, this can create a problem. It is one of those things that requires judgment on your part. If substance abuse is bound to come up in a background or reference check, or if the application required you to acknowledge the problem, take the initiative and explain that you have solved it. If your drinking was a very private thing that is not apt to be passed along by others, you may want to let the matter pass unless you are asked.

Smoking can pose an interesting challenge for a candidate. In what is increasingly a nonsmokers' world, it can be an emotional issue for you or the interviewer. If the interviewer is a smoker, she or he will probably have the discipline not to do so with you—even at lunch. If the interviewer asks whether you mind if she or he has a cigarette, you have to make a judgment call. The best response may be to say that you are not a smoker, but have no objection to the interviewer's smoking. Be sensitive, make your point that smoking is not your thing—but don't get on your soapbox. If you are the smoker, definitely forget it unless your interviewer is a smoker, too, and you can both light up without offending others. While many people wouldn't say so openly, they would not hire a smoker if it could be avoided. If you are working on breaking the habit, say so. If you expect to smoke only on your breaks outside the office, say so. If smoking is of emotional importance to you, you may have a problem in many contemporary offices.

ACCEPTING DIFFERENT PERSONALITIES

Be ready to accept a contrasting personality when you meet your interviewer. It isn't necessary that you be of the same ilk to get along well together. Tolerance should be your byword as you interview with a company. Expect to meet different kinds of people, and make up your mind ahead of time that you are going to accept those differences.

SENIORS INTERVIEWED BY JUNIORS

Age or experience differences shouldn't separate you from your interviewer. While there are many potentially awkward combinations, let's assume that you are a senior person interviewing with a relatively junior human resources officer. It may be necessary for you to set the mood by being relaxed and pleasantly respectful of your interviewer's position. Keep the interview an objective business affair with a natural extension of the kinds of friendly interaction you would have with a similarly experienced person anywhere else in life. Be nice. Take care of business. Avoid resenting the gap in age and experience, and make your interview a positive experience for both of you—instead of an unspoken contest over who should be interviewing whom based on the merits.

SEXUAL CHEMISTRY

Another area of human interaction that is no stranger to the employment interview is sexual chemistry—pleasant and unpleasant. Chapter 9 deals with the topic more thoroughly, but you should not be surprised if it happens. There are gracious and effective ways to keep it from becoming a problem, except in the most extreme cases.

Using Your Research

You made an effort to research the company, the position, and the people you might meet or discuss at your interview. Now is the time to use your research. The trick to doing so effectively is letting it enter into the dialogue naturally and incrementally. It has to flow and complement points that would normally be made anyway. The exception is when you have an opportunity to ask a question that can use new information as its basis. That is an acceptable way of opening new lines of inquiry and ideal for exhibiting your knowledge of the company.

SHOWING INTEREST IN THE COMPANY

Your starting point for showing interest in the company and the job is in demonstrating a clear understanding of what it does—and what you expect to contribute. This is a two-sided proposition. You want to be cautious about your interests appearing to be too narrow. Use the following general guidelines. Dispense your company knowledge incrementally and naturally. Take your time and let the interviewer set the stage for how specific you can safely become.

As the situation is drawn more clearly by the interviewer, use your answers—and questions—to show your company knowledge, working your assets into a plausible model for satisfying the company's needs.

Guidelines for Showing Company Knowledge

- Mention specific instances where the company has been successful—or unsuccessful—and how your skills and sensitivities could have contributed to or changed the outcome.

- If you know the key personalities of the organization, associate yourself with the winners, distance yourself from the losers—all in the course of the interview and in such a way as to come across a candid observer rather than an all-knowing critic.

- Have alternative solutions for each problem—make these positive, and position the company as the beneficiary, with you profiting only as a member of the team.

- Respectfully subordinate yourself to the organization, and don't come across as a one-person act with an answer for everything.

- Pose as an aware observer with some tentative theories about how things work at the company, but with humility and respect for the knowledge of the insiders.

- Appear interested, aware, and anxious to test your preliminary solutions with people in a position to give you the feedback needed to make them realistic.

LEARNING ABOUT THE JOB

Use your knowledge of the company and its people to find out exactly what the employer wants to accomplish by filling this position. If your network and research have given you incomplete or conflicting readings about this, now is the time for clarifications. Do it early in the interview, because you run the risk of exhibiting faulty knowledge. Also, the earlier in the interview you do it, the better positioned you are to use the remaining time making your case for why you are the person to hire.

IDENTIFY THE DECISION MAKER

You want to identify the decision maker as soon as possible. Your ability to sort differing opinions of the job and the priorities surrounding it can be crucial to your hiring. It is not uncommon for the boss to expose you to others on staff who obviously have differing approaches to the problem. When it comes time to interview with the boss, you can expect to be asked your own opinion as to the most productive solution. Choosing his or her direction, or making a sensitive case for not doing so, is important. By questioning others in the interview chain before reaching the decision maker, you can have the information you need to react intelligently. Keep in mind that the right answer doesn't always agree with what you know to be the favorite solution. If in your interview with the boss you have made sense out of differing staff opinions, you have gained more than you would have with an obedient answer. Be willing to take a well-reasoned risk in situations that let you demonstrate your ability to distill information into an original solution. The technique is illustrated in Case History 9.

Save the salary questions for later. It is the one thing about the job you don't want to pursue at this stage. Again, you face the problem of casting yourself too narrowly. If you place an emphasis on salary early in the selection process, you make it a premature priority for both sides in the hiring. You risk forcing early closure on an issue that deserves to stay flexible until your real value is apparent. Case History 10 shows you how to handle the situation.

SHOWING INTEREST IN YOUR INTERVIEWER

In addition to approaching your interviewer as a potential friend instead of an adversary, this is the time to apply any knowledge you've gained that might strengthen your relationship. If your research revealed an article he or she wrote, mention having read it. If she or he has things in his or her office that betray a common interest—for example, aviation—share the interest honestly. Don't overdo it, but use the occasion to express respect for the avocation. Use knowledge of your interviewer to personalize the relationship early. It will give you a better platform for selling yourself as the right person to hire. You create an expectation of good things to come, and that can be helpful. Case History 11 shows you how.

Dealing with Questions

Your greatest influence on the interview's outcome is in how you deal with the questions you are asked. What you say is important, but so is how you say it—demonstrating your poise and ability to think under stress is as much a part of the process as the objective questions and answers. Here are some guidelines that you should be familiar with and use to your advantage:

Basic Rules for Handling Questions

- Learn as much about the job as possible so you can answer questions in the proper context and steer the interview toward your strengths.

- Pay attention to the interviewer, and be ready to react to her or his interests, rather than concentrating on a rigid agenda of your own.

- Expect more than one-word answers and stock interviewer questions—be prepared for questions that require you to be more expansive.

- Be ready to appraise your own job performance, give reasons for your opinions, and tell how you accomplished specific things.

Case History 9—Situation

SOLVING A PROBLEM AT YOUR INTERVIEW

Background

Bob McClay is a successful group sales specialist with a major national insurance company. ❶ He is tired of frequent travel and is seeking a partnership interest in a hometown agency where he and his bride plan to relocate and raise a family. His background is impressive, but he is going to have to ❷ make a special impression to jump from sales representative to partner.

Situation

Bob enters his interview with the senior partner of Edgewright Agency as he finishes ❸ a day of informal interviews with several key people. As he takes his seat and they make the transition from small talk to substantive issues, his prospective boss and partner asks, "Well, Bob, if you're going to own a hunk of this business, ❹ you're going to have to deal with its problems. You've been around for a few hours now. Which one do you suggest tackling first?" ❺ While he is a little surprised by the question, Bob ❻ recalls a few things that seemed to have the staff perplexed. ❼ One of them was the onslaught of out-of-the-region telephone solicitations to certain segments of their traditional client base. He decides to place ❽ sales and service above operational matters and makes this his problem to solve. "Mr. Edgewright, your folks are having a problem bucking the telemarketers from Pennsylvania. Just getting defensive about it isn't going to make things better—and that's the main response I was hearing today. ❾ I have an idea about local telemarketing that I'd like to develop for you." And Bob goes on to introduce the local agency to a kind of marketing that suits its situation very well but was not something the agency had thought of trying. His experience with the technique on the national level makes him the perfect person to lead in that new direction.

Conclusion

Bob ❿ enters the interview an outside observer and leaves it on the verge of becoming an inside problem solver. An opportunity is presented that vaults him beyond his resume and puts his abilities to work in a way that matters to the bottom line. He can do more than close sales; he is also partnership material.

Case History 9—Analysis

SOLVING A PROBLEM AT YOUR INTERVIEW

General Strategy

Bob comes into the interview with a sixth sense that says, "I've got to become a player here right away if I am to become a partner. Otherwise I'm going to be what I've already been—a salesman." He looks for his opening and finds it when the senior partner asks his opinion on something he can make a contribution to directly.

Specific Points

❶ Lifestyle changes can alter your career path—a job interview is often one of the first places that you realize how significant the change will be.

❷ When you are attempting to make a significant impact on top management, it helps to be in a position to "fix something"—be ready to solve a problem.

❸ Your interview day often begins with the "lesser lights" and ends with the boss. Appreciate the difference in how you should perform in each setting.

❹ Expect a blockbuster. He or she assumes you've already covered the routine things with others.

❺ When you aspire to a role that is different from that of the regular employees, expect questions that reflect values different from those they reflected.

❻ Be a keen observer and listener in the preliminary interviews in order to be prepared to make a contribution if the opportunity presents itself.

❼ Pick a problem that seems to lack an in-house solution.

❽ Given a choice, go for the bottom-line issues, not the organizational or philosophical ones.

❾ Present your tentative solution and make it clear that you don't presume to solve it on the spot—entice the boss to hear the rest of your story as a partner.

❿ The task is to change your image from that of an outside observer into a problem solver intimately involved in structuring a real solution.

- Understand the reason for open-ended questions and other techniques used to prolong your responses in hopes of gaining more depth; use them to amplify your strengths and promote your own agenda.

- Be an attentive listener; it will give you a chance to read the situation and adjust your strategy to the dynamics of the interview, not just react.

- Use hypothetical questions about how you would solve problems as opportunities to project your strengths and show awareness of the company's needs, how it operates, and how you can make a contribution.

- Be ready for surprise questions like, "We all have things we'd rather not have known about us. What is there in your background that you'd rather tell us about now than have discovered later?" (See Chapter 2 on how to respond.)

If you know these rules, you are better prepared than the average candidate. They put you in the enviable position of having been "taught the test." You are freed from the anxiety of wondering what is happening during your interview. You can face the interviewer's questions calmly and frame the kinds of responses that leave a favorable impression—both in style and substance. As important, perhaps, you can avoid the traps that have been laid out for you. With your thorough knowledge of questioning procedures, you can sidestep the awkward moments and focus the interviewer's attention on what you have to offer.

BEHAVIORAL INTERVIEWING

Business Week's John Byrne reported that "behavioral interviewing" is the in thing for human resources experts and personnel consultants from coast to coast who now stress finding out what a person is going to do on the job, not just verifying that he or she has the credentials to do it. The article quoted Jim Kennedy of San Francisco's Management Team Consultants, who says you can expect four categories of questioning in a behavioral interview:

- **Problem question.** "Give me an example of a problem in which you and your manager disagreed over how to accomplish a goal."

- **Continuum question.** "Do your talents lean more toward strategy or tactics, being creative or analytical?"

- **Comparison question.** "How would you compare, say, the marketing of consumer goods versus financial services?"

- **Future question.** "A year from now, what might your boss say during a performance review about your work for the company?"

Each of these questions is designed to draw you out and make you demonstrate your ability to deal with problems, show your strengths and weaknesses, and help interviewers judge whether you have the skills and personal characteristics that will make you a successful transfer into their organization. Review them and practice changing the wording and settings to suit your own professional situation. Rehearse the kinds of answers you might give, and be ready to respond with ease if you are faced with this new interviewing technique.

ADJUSTING TO THE INTERVIEWER'S REACTION

As your interview progresses, it is up to you to appraise the impact your answers are having and calibrate your subsequent responses accordingly. You can compare this to an artillery battery firing early rounds and having a spotter near the target call back instructions for improving accuracy. In the interview, you have to be your own spotter and look for clues for adjusting the interview in the face, words, and body language of your interviewer.

You have several choices on how to make your adjustments. If the response is positive, continue in the same vein. If the interviewer is getting bored and appears just to be going through the motions, you have nothing to lose by livening up the interview with a more controversial answer. Judgment is needed not to go from bad to worse, but the right move can save you. If you can break the monotony in some positive way, you are ahead of the game.

LISTENING, UNDERSTANDING, AND CLARIFYING

You need to settle down and listen to what is going on around you during your interview. If you are too rehearsed, nervous, or insensitive to the signals being sent, you might miss important cues from your interviewer. Often the interviewer will signal the kind of response that is wanted—all you have to do is be alert enough to receive the message. If you find yourself receiving mixed or unclear signals, or just don't understand the question, ask for clarification. If you need time to compose your thoughts, ask the interviewer to clarify his or her question.

TAKING TIME TO THINK

You don't have to give an instant response. It is expected that you might need to pause for a moment to think about what is being asked. You can actually create a negative impression by immediately shooting back an answer every time, suggesting that you are so heavily rehearsed as to leave no room for an original thought, or that you don't think the question is worthy of serious thought. In either case you

Case History 10—Situation

DELAYING THE SALARY QUESTION

Background

Wanda McFee is a landscape architect ❶ making the transition from working in the public sector on a scaled government salary to a position with a commercial developer. Part of her motivation is financial, and ❷ she wants to establish her value objectively and not on the basis of what she currently earns.

Situation

Wanda is going for an interview with the head of exterior design for a leading developer of commercial properties in a major city. ❸ She is well qualified for the position advertised and even has experience with government projects of a similar magnitude. As her interview progresses, ❹ she is asked the salary question early on. "Ms. McFee, ❺ we like the qualifications you're bringing to the position. What do you think it would take to retain you?" the interviewer asks. ❻ "Thank you for recognizing my potential, Mr. Smith, and I'm sure XYZ Development has a salary in mind that would be more than competitive for the work to be done." ❼ Other questions of a general nature follow; then the interviewer returns to salary: "What are you currently earning as a GS-12 with the Park Service?" he asks. ❽ "Well, GS-12s are paid in a range from $22,000 to $38,000, and I've been in the system for quite a few years." More general questions; then: "Frankly, Miss McKee, I need to establish whether we can afford you. Can you tell me your financial expectations?" he asks. "I don't have a dollar figure per se, but it would help me to know what XYZ normally expects to pay a person with the responsibilities we've discussed this afternoon. ❾ What do you plan to offer someone in my situation?" she responds. "We have a range that runs from the mid-$30s to upper $40s, depending on the circumstances," he answers. "I see no reason why we can't reach a suitable figure when an offer is made," she says as the topic changes.

Conclusion

Wanda wants to avoid having the developer add 15 percent to her government salary and bring her in at a low salary. ❿ She dances around the increasingly direct questions until he is satisfied that, short of insisting, he is going to get nothing but agreement that they are within each other's range.

Case History 10—Analysis

DELAYING THE SALARY QUESTION

General Strategy

Wanda needs to walk the narrow line between being obstinate and acting in her own best interests. She does that by turning the interviewer's questions into generalized responses, loosely defined ranges, and questions of her own.

Specific Points

❶ Your salary expectations can differ when changing categories of employer.

❷ In such a situation you want to avoid having your future salary determined solely by your past salary in a lower-paying industry.

❸ Your best strategy for a fair salary adjustment is to focus on your qualifications, not past salary, so prepare to put emphasis on the potential employer's compensation standard, not on your old salary.

❹ An early attempt to get you to name a salary figure should not be unexpected, but a definitive response is unnecessary.

❺ This is a "buy signal"—the interviewer wants to hire you. It is your license to dance a little on the salary question.

❻ Begin with appreciation and end by stating your expectation that they will treat the salary question fairly.

❼ It is common practice for the interviewer to back off on the salary question and then revisit it a few minutes later.

❽ Don't try to make a secret out of public information, but you can avoid telling precisely where you stand and probably get away with it.

❾ If you have the opportunity, shift the question back to the interviewer—chances are you will end up stating overlapping scales and leave the figure for later negotiations, as it should be.

❿ While a totally insistent inquiry should get an honest answer, most salary questions early in the interview can satisfactorily end with a defined range.

Case History 11—Situation

SHOWING INTEREST IN YOUR INTERVIEWER

Background

Barry Warren is a library technician looking for his ❶ first permanent position after working as a student assistant during four years of undergraduate study. He has his basic credentials and clearly relevant student work experience, but what will ❷ make the difference in a competitive interviewing situation against similar candidates is finding a basis for standing out positively in the mind of his interviewer.

Situation

Barry appears for his interview with a little bit of ❸ apprehension about the person scheduled to conduct it. He will be interviewed by the woman who used to supervise him as a student intern at the college library. Even though this is quite a different setting, a large municipal library, he ❹ remembers her as a distant person he never felt he knew. "Good morning, Mr. Warren," she begins. "I see we have something in common." ❺ Assuming she was referring to the college library, he answers, "Yes, we spent some hours together in the professional reference division at State College." "That's true enough, ❻ but I was thinking more along the lines of gemstones—I see you're wearing sapphire cuff links and a class ring. The stone must mean something to you!" she concludes. Caught off guard, he forgets about libraries entirely for a moment and ❼ enters into a lively discussion of gem- and birthstones. She points out a mounted set of specimens she has treasured since her college days, and they enjoy a few moments of ❽ talk that only gem collectors could possibly appreciate. It sets the stage for what is ❾ otherwise a routine interview. But it establishes that his experience, training, and aspirations suit the position well.

Conclusion

Barry is fortunate enough to stumble on a common interest with his interviewer that serves as an ice breaker and basis for identifying with each other. ❿ Without it he and the otherwise dissimilar interviewer may have failed to connect in any meaningful way, and the job might have gone to someone else.

Case History 11—Analysis

SHOWING INTEREST IN YOUR INTERVIEWER

General Strategy

Barry realizes that his credentials for the job are adequate but not outstanding. He hopes to find some spark of common interest with his interviewer so he will stand out from other candidates. While he knows of no such link, when it is presented he seizes on the opportunity and shares her appreciation of a hobby.

Specific Points

❶ First positions in particular are helped by common interests between interviewer and applicant because there is no great base of professional experience to share.

❷ You are looking for some comfortable way to stand out in a field of similar candidates, any of whom could do the job.

❸ Apprehension is normal in interviews, and you need to acknowledge it but be ready for positive developments.

❹ Try to remove past impressions when you interview with a previous acquaintance. Be ready to see something new in the interviewer.

❺ It would not have been Barry's place to shift to a nonprofessional topic even if he had noticed the collection of gemstones.

❻ But when the interviewer gives an entrée, you are free to join the off-the-topic discussion and promote the mutual interest.

❼ Since the opening was provided, it is perfectly appropriate to follow the line of discussion at the interviewer's invitation.

❽ Shared language or specialized vocabulary is one of the quickest ways to establish commonality between yourself and an interviewer.

❾ An interview that had little promise beyond ordinary fact verification has taken on shades that will make Barry memorable at decision time.

❿ Unless revealed by your research, interests are usually spontaneous, and you just have to be ready to develop them as they appear.

stand a chance of impressing your interviewer negatively. Even if you are ready with an immediate comeback, show respect for the question, give it a pensive moment, then answer. The interviewer wants to think that she or he has caused you to think and has elicited the best you have to give, not an immediate reaction. Judgment is always necessary, and you have to vary your pattern to keep things interesting.

DELIBERATELY DIFFICULT QUESTIONS

Some interviewers deliberately put you on the spot with questions like:

- "We all have things we'd rather not have known about us. What is there in your background that you'd rather tell us about now than have it discovered later?"
- "Tell me what kinds of things you and your last boss used to fight about."
- "What do you consider to be your greatest weakness professionally?"

Be ready for the surprise question. (See Chapter 2 for further advice.) It doesn't always come, but when it does, your best weapon against it is sidestepping the expected shock; don't fall into the trap of an embarrassed confession that is neither necessary nor expected. Be composed, think for a moment, and respond in some inoffensively circumspect way that deals with the question safely and demonstrates your ability to cope with surprise. Case History 12 illustrates how to deal with difficult questions.

STANDING YOUR GROUND

It isn't necessary for you to be a doormat during your interview. If the interviewer is aggressive in his or her questioning, field the questions as objectively and unemotionally as you can. If something is offensive or wrong, defend your position as graciously as you can, then ask what the question is intended to reveal. Is there some suspected problem that you might better discuss more directly? Express your willingness—your preference—to do so in a forthright manner instead of risking misunderstandings by innuendo. Don't go looking for a fight, but if the interview is clearly in jeopardy, you have little to lose by challenging the line of questioning and then offering your full cooperation if there is a problem that needs to be addressed. Case History 13 shows you how this can be done.

MOTIVES FOR QUESTIONS

Your reaction to a question often depends on why you think it is being asked. A seemingly hostile question can be taken in stride if you understand the interviewer's motivation. Put yourself in the interviewer's position and imagine why she or he might take a certain tack in the questioning. Usually you will be able to see the reason and lend your cooperation without emotion or offense. Sometimes the interviewer will actually end a line of required difficult questions with the disclaimer "You know those are things we have to ask." Generally speaking, you are better advised to tolerate the questioning and realize that it is just part of the process of testing you for the position. Assume the question is relevant to the job and do your best to answer unless the question is clearly improper or damaging.

AVOIDING NEGATIVE COMMENTS ABOUT OTHERS

The fastest way to turn a former nemesis into an object of sympathy is to malign the person, making him or her the reason for your failure in a former position. Be objective and positive about the people with whom you have shared your career. It goes without saying that you've had your differences with people. Your interview for a new position is no time to stress this. If there was ever a time to look for the silver lining, be charitable, magnanimous, and forgiving of human frailties, this is it.

Future employers want to hire team players. People who can get along with others are in demand; those who can't, aren't. You should emphasize two characteristics for the new employer:

- your ability to learn from your mistakes; and
- your ability to put unpleasant things behind you.

Satisfy the curiosity of your interviewer with as much objective detail as necessary, and then set your focus on the future. If you possibly can, formally make peace with the person who was the problem in your former position and offer him or her as a willing "negative reference"—someone who will say you had your differences but were essentially a competent worker. The best ending for a bad incident in your career is healing the wound and letting the past sleep. Case History 14 illustrates how you might do this.

Case History 12—Situation

DEALING WITH DIFFICULT QUESTIONS

Background

Susan O'Hare is a pharmacist who is looking for a position with a supermarket chain after being fired from her last position ❶ after only a few months on the job. She is well qualified and has an excellent record as a retail pharmacist prior to ❷ the unfortunate incident that ended her last employment. Difficult questions are expected as she interviews for a position she hopes will put the whole thing behind her.

Situation

Susan enters the office confidently and takes her place across the desk from the woman who will question her. She makes easy conversation as the interview begins in earnest. Everything is relaxed until she is asked the question ❸ she was beginning to think would never come. "You were let go from your last position, Ms. O'Hare. ❹ Tell me about it," her interviewer inquires. "I was fired after a personal misunderstanding with the manager of the store where I worked," she explains, ❺ hoping it will end there. "What kind of 'personal misunderstanding' would be serious enough to cost you your job?" the interviewer asks, pressing the point. ❻ "I was being sexually harassed," she replies without elaborating. "And YOU got fired?" the interviewer asks, implying that it should have been the other way around. ❼ "I couldn't prove it—it was his word against mine. When I became an embarrassment, he made my working situation difficult and terminated me without cause as my probation period was about to end," she explains. ❽ The incident was one that didn't lend itself to a fully objective resolution, so Susan only reluctantly elaborated when asked specific questions about it and ❾ turned the conversation toward the contributions she hoped to make to this organization if given the opportunity.

Conclusion

Susan is in the difficult position of not wanting to dwell on a negative incident or speak ill of a past employer. But ❿ she has to explain something that mars her record and damages her employability. The best approach is to tell the truth and show her intention to put the problem behind her.

Case History 12—Analysis

DEALING WITH DIFFICULT QUESTIONS

General Strategy

Susan knows that her last period of employment is too brief to be explained in any positive way. She decides to let the interviewer ask for an explanation and to provide the details in as limited and unemotional terms as she can. Her plan is to confront the incident directly without more elaboration than necessary. She will honestly tell her side of the story and place the focus on the future, not the past.

Specific Points

❶ Brief tenure in a position can be expected to bring on tough questions if there is no accompanying explanation.

❷ Incidents such as unsubstantiated sexual harassment are difficult to express routinely in a resume or cover letter, so they are left for the interview.

❸ Interviewers often hold back the hard questions to see if they are made unnecessary by other developments in the course of the interview.

❹ This is the kind of open-ended question that puts you in a position to give the incident the tone you feel it deserves.

❺ It is worth trying a generic explanation if you would prefer not to delve into an unpleasant situation, but be prepared for more pressing questions.

❻ A direct and simple statement of the problem is better than an emotional diatribe, if you can honestly be that objective.

❼ Honesty and realism are your best defenses in fielding difficult questions.

❽ Understand that unprovable conflicts are best handled by as much calm distancing as you can muster—you can never prove the case, so just tell it your way and rise above the clouded issues.

❾ As you explain the negative past, try to project a positive future.

❿ Make your case without letting the incident brand you as a wrongfully terminated but troubled worker who is risky to hire.

Case History 13—Situation

```
STANDING YOUR GROUND
WHEN YOU HAVE TO
```

Background

Sam Boyd is the resident manager of a condominium complex and a candidate for a prestigious new project in another part of the country. **❶** He expects tough questioning on his role in converting the last property from a rental into a condominium property. It is the kind of questioning he has faced before, and while his answers are ready, so is his **❷** willingness to defend his position.

Situation

Sam is met by the marketing vice president. She tells him that he is to meet with her and several other senior managers. They arrive at the sales office, **❸** he takes the tour, and the interview begins. They **❹** begin to probe the sensitive area of handling conversions—the slow real estate market is **❺** forcing them to rent many of the units initially and convert them to condos later. "Sam, we know you've been through the conversion wars—**❻** you and K-Group got a lot of bad press. Would you do the same thing to us?" one of them asks. **❼** "No one plans to get 'bad press' and, no, I wouldn't want to repeat the experience," Sam responds. **❽** "But that's how you got the job done there, isn't it?" the marketing VP asks. "If you are saying that we won by fighting the battle against rent control, yes," he answers. "No, I read it as more than that—you headed a group that busted the tenant organization at any price in spite of the image loss!" she continues. **❾** "It sounds like you have something more direct to say to me—please just say it and let me respond. I have a well-documented record through a difficult period that I'll be happy to explain and let you verify with third parties," Sam urges, positioning himself to respond objectively and not get into an argument about appearances.

Conclusion

Sam could **❿** continue responding to individual barbs about his controversial role in the conversion project; instead he confronts the veiled hostility and pleads for an objective evaluation of the public record.

Case History 13—Analysis

STANDING YOUR GROUND WHEN YOU HAVE TO

General Strategy

Sam knows innuendo will be part of his interview—the press paints him as a ruthless tenant property manager. He wants to retain the reputation of an effective businessman capable of dealing with tenant/landlord issues but be seen fairly, not as someone who will trash the company's reputation while accomplishing its objectives. He is willing to confront the issue if necessary.

Specific Points

❶ In this case, Sam knows that he is in for tough questioning.

❷ If the questioning gets out of line, Sam plans to control the issue by bringing it into open discussion.

❸ Often the ride in from the airport or the preliminary tour provides clues as to the tone of the interview.

❹ A pet issue will surface that is both of vital interest and troubling to the interviewers.

❺ Economic conditions are forcing this group to consider tactics they had hoped to avoid, and Sam is taking the brunt of their discomfort.

❻ The interview drifts away from the problem and focuses on an incident in Sam's past.

❼ Sam acknowledges the difficulty and tries to let the issue rest.

❽ The interview gets accusatory, and they trade increasingly different perspectives on the issue.

❾ Sam seizes the opportunity to end the drift toward an argumentative interview and gives it a positive spin by suggesting third-party verifications.

❿ An entire interview can be spent dancing around hidden agenda items that should be confronted. The candidate sometimes has more to gain by forcing the issue.

Interview Psychology

Psychology is the science of explaining human behavior. Interviewing for a job is an exercise in using your knowledge of human behavior to influence an employer's opinion of you favorably. The employer does the same to sell you on his or her company. Plus the interviewer assesses how you will probably react to various questions and situations to judge what kind of person you are. Your job interview is a two-sided experience in applied psychology. Here are some of the fundamental things you should keep in mind as you become a player in this exchange and measurement of behavior known as the employment interview.

TECHNIQUES USED BY INTERVIEWERS

The kinds of interviews identified in Chapter 2 are showcases for the interviewers' psychological techniques. Most interviews are of the unstructured, informal variety where neither side invokes much in the way of identifiable psychological manipulation. A few techniques, such as the stress interview, are deliberately designed psychological tests of how you behave when forced into certain situations. Group and panel interviews are also psychological in nature to the extent that they force you to react to a contrived situation. Most interviewing psychology is less deliberate, and two people test one another for compatibility and likability—shared values that will allow them to work harmoniously together.

You might encounter more formal applications of psychology in the hiring cycle and find the results introduced into the interview. For example, you may have been asked to take a formal test that measures your personality, honesty, or some other attribute relevant to your employment. In some instances, prospective employees are interviewed by a professional psychologist. Chapter 6 discusses the technology used in interviewing and includes a look at psychological testing.

PERSONALITY AND THE JOB INTERVIEW

Since your interview is with another human being, the chances are good that it will be with a personality different from your own. That matters for two reasons:

- You will be interacting with someone who places importance on things differently from how you might, and

- Your personality will be, at least informally, typed as suitable or unsuitable for the job offered.

While the literature of popular psychology is filled with schemes for attaching catchy names to the differences in people's personalities, Dr. John Holland of Johns Hopkins University has made a science of relating personality types to careers. Here are six personality types, abstracted by the author, which Dr. Holland has observed:

1. *Realistic*—unsociable, emotionally stable, materialistic, genuine, concrete, and oriented to the present.

2. *Intellectual*—analytical, rational, independent, radical, abstract, introverted, cognitive, critical, curious, and perceptive.

3. *Social*—sociable, nurturing, dominant, and psychologically oriented.

4. *Conventional*—well-controlled, neat, sociable, inflexible, conservative, persevering, stereotyped, practical, correct, lacks spontaneity and originality.

5. *Enterprising*—adventurous, dominant, enthusiastic, energetic, impulsive, persuasive, verbal, extroverted, self-accepting, self-confident, orally aggressive, exhibitionist.

6. *Artistic*—complex outlook, independent judgment, introverted, original, subjective, imaginative, expressive, interpretive, fantasy-oriented.

The main relevance of this model to job interviewing is in showing you how very different people are. You can benefit by entering your interview with an appreciation of the breadth of possible values you might encounter. It can help you account for people's motivation. You need to appreciate that we are each a blend of the personality types that Dr. Holland factored into six separate entities for the purpose of studying them. In reality, you are expected to be more than a single type—and those with whom you must deal in the interview (and later the workplace) will be equally complex human beings. All of that is to say, have an appreciation for personality differences but don't allow yourself to be short-circuited for a position that seems right or wrong for you because of a superficial appearance of incompatible personalities. The science is imprecise, and you should view personality as only one more indicator in making your vocational choice.

HIDDEN AGENDAS

Psychological awareness can help you understand another fundamental of human behavior that will likely be operating during your job interview. People and their questions are not always what they seem to be. Each of us can selectively misrepresent our true intentions to accomplish something else. In job interviewing, the hir-

Case History 14—Situation

DEALING WITH PAST NEGATIVE EXPERIENCES

Background

Connie Williams is an assistant manager in an upscale suburban shopping mall boutique. She is a ❶ candidate for manager at a similar concession in the anchor department store in the same complex. Her interview may reveal that she had a ❷ minor criminal conviction some years ago for being in the wrong place at the wrong time. She plans to explain if asked, but not volunteer the information.

Situation

Connie is met by Ted Jensen, who invites her to be seated for their interview. ❸ The usual questions are asked and everything goes well. She is asked if there are any questions she would like to ask of him and takes the occasion to clarify a few things. ❹ As the interview nears its conclusion, Mr. Jensen asks, ❺ "Connie, is there anything you would like to tell me about yourself that we haven't discussed? Something you'd rather mention now rather than have it come to light at a later time?" Instead of baring her soul, ❻ Connie looks at him and asks if there is something he has in mind. His response is, ❼ "Yes, there is. We do routine background checks on our candidates, and yours showed a conviction." ❽ "Let me tell you about that," she continues. "More than ten years ago I was dating a guy who meant more to me than he should have. I went places with him that I shouldn't have. One night he got arrested for drug possession and I couldn't clear my name—my attorney recommended accepting the misdemeanor and putting it behind me. My life before and after is clear of any wrongdoing." "Why didn't you mention it?" he inquires. ❾ "Because it is a small incident from a long time ago. I was hoping it had passed," she answers.

Conclusion

Connie tries to have her interview on the merits of her present life ❿ but runs into an incident from the past. When confronted she gives a reasonable explanation but feels no obligation to damage her image forever by citing a small negative that has little relevance to what she is today and wants to become.

Case History 14—Analysis

DEALING WITH PAST NEGATIVE EXPERIENCES

General Strategy

Connie knows there is a possibility that an employer check will reveal a minor criminal conviction from her past. She decides that there is more to be gained by distancing herself from the incident than from volunteering the information. If confronted, she will give a completely truthful explanation and express the understandable desire to let it fade.

Specific Points

❶ Managing a retail store is the kind of job that logically could produce a criminal-record check.

❷ Since the charge did not involve mishandling money or anything directly relevant to retail management, she decides not to volunteer the information.

❸ A minor conviction like Connie's might be used to eliminate an otherwise undesirable candidate, but her overall record was good.

❹ The timing of such an inquiry could be different, but coming at the end of the interview is common.

❺ "Is there anything you'd like to tell me..." can be phrased many ways, but it is an open invitation to tell all that you feel is relevant.

❻ An acceptable and still limited response is to ask the interviewer if there is something he has in mind.

❼ The worst case is that he does have something that you might have mentioned.

❽ And when that is the case, you are not startled by it but prepared to tell your story.

❾ If pressed, you explain that mentioning the incident is something you just don't do—and surely they can understand why.

❿ Put the entire incident in the context of a total life that is otherwise positive.

ing official's hidden agenda while interviewing you might be to find flaws that justify hiring a friend instead. Her or his outward agenda is the objective evaluation of your qualities relative to the position.

All hidden agenda actions are not so sinister. The practice can take the form of seemingly off-the-subject questions that actually form a legitimate evaluation for an important job success criterion. Your task is to recognize what is going on and still make your case as you respond. If you are unaware of the hidden agenda phenomenon, you can be lulled into thinking that your interviewer is wandering off the point when he or she is actually zeroing in quite deliberately on your suitability for the job.

DEALING WITH STRESS

Putting you under deliberate stress has already been mentioned as a specific interview technique. You are more apt to encounter it as a less deliberate adjunct to the interviewing process. Stage personalities have long credited nervous anticipation with ultimately energizing their performances. Their secret is in harnessing the energy—acknowledging that it exists and deliberately channeling it toward a useful end. You can do the same thing at your job interview. No one is going to tell you that stressful feelings can be eliminated, but they can be controlled and directed toward supporting your effort instead of detracting from it.

The first thing you can do to reduce the stress of your job interview is to prepare thoroughly. But don't overdo it. Perfection is not your goal, and trying to reach it can be stress-producing in itself. Follow the guidance of the first three chapters of this book and you will have anticipated 90 percent of the your interview's potential surprises. With them removed, let the remaining 10 percent add spontaneity to your interview. Go in well prepared and realistic about the fact that there will still be challenges that you will have to respond to on the spot. Not to have such residual unknowns would deny you the opportunity to show off your ability to think on your feet. Welcome the opportunity rather than dread it.

The other things you can do to reduce stress include getting rest; having a positive, realistic attitude about the whole interviewing process; and coming to the session feeling good about your physical condition and appearance. There are both physical and mental exercises that some people find helpful when facing stressful situations. Most of them boil down to giving you an alternative point of concentration—you occupy your mind with calm thoughts of something other than the interview. Some people use their religious faith in this regard. For the more secular there are books and tapes on the subject of managing stressful feelings. If stress is an unusually threatening problem for you, investigate the popular literature at your library or bookstore.

BODY LANGUAGE

While you sometimes find more credit given to the phenomenon of body language than it deserves, there is something to it. The way a person physically postures probably does communicate something that has an impact on others. If you are aware of the potential for sending the right or the wrong message, you can discipline yourself to communicating only the one you intend.

Translating and Controlling Body Language

- Follow your host's lead as you go through the ritual of meeting—accept his or her handshake firmly, but only when offered, or you risk coming across as too aggressive and dominant. The same rule applies to seating—let your host suggest the location and time to be seated. Mirror the interviewer's greeting expressions, such as the traditional smile and uplifting of the eyebrows—naturally, of course, not affected.

- Respect personal space—arm's length is comfortable for most people. Crowding your host is uncomfortable and signals an intrusive personality that can be awkward or difficult to deal with on the job. A forward-leaning gesture is positive; a forward move into the personal space is not.

- Being attentive and interested is largely shown with the eyes—"natural" is the key word. Avoid extremes of looking away, staring, blinking or not blinking, or closing your eyes—anything other than what you would do in regular social or business discourse. It shows insecurity and an inability to handle this special situation. The same is true of facial muscle tension as manifested in eyebrow positioning, smiles, tight lipline, etc.—breathe deeply a few times, relax, and be natural. Tell yourself that the interviewer likes you, and picture him or her as a friend, but not an overly familiar one! Be careful how you fix your gaze if the interviewer is an attractive member of the opposite sex—there are all kinds of possibilities for inappropriate communication there.

- Nervous bobbing of the head indicates impatience to get on to the next topic. Slow the same gesture down a bit and you show agreement and interest.

- Gestures should be open and uplifting, whether it is your arms, posture, smile, or other facial feature—up is usually associated with positive and winning, down with defeat and negative things. Crossed or folded arms is a closed gesture and is viewed as protective instead of welcoming. Even crossed legs and ankles are said to connote stubbornness. Showing your palms on occasion as you gesture is a sign of openness, nothing to hide.

- A naturally invoked and periodically used gesture is better than a constant one—a fixed smile appears artificial; a spontaneous one, genuine.

- Nervousness and discomfort show on your face in how you position your mouth, touching it frequently or clearing your throat too often or on cue when you are put on the spot—all come across as insincere and unnatural, the opposite of what the interviewer wants to see.

- Avoid doing nervous things such as tugging at your clothing (tie, collar, etc.) or distracting ones such as fidgeting, tapping your foot, or anything else that breaks the desired image of control and poise you want to convey.

- Smugness is to be avoided, too—overly familiar or relaxed gestures such as crossed hands behind the head, the "wrong" kind of smile, an all-knowing look and demeanor maintained throughout your interview, extended legs crossed at the ankles, and hands on hips and thumbs in belt are all potentially read as inappropriate dominance.

- Slow is better; when in doubt, take your time in deliberately executing any gesture—again, not artificially so, but don't rush and convey nervousness or anxiety.

- Finally, don't become paranoid about the magic of body language. While these points are worth considering, forget about molding them into some contrived pattern of presenting yourself—your own natural state will come across better than stilted conformity to "rules" you read in some book. If you can incorporate them into your routine, do it. If you have to fight to achieve the image you want, forget it and be you.

POSITIVE EXPECTATIONS

As you go into your interview, try to keep the whole thing in perspective. It is important, but it is not a life-and-death situation for you. At the very least, this interview will be a learning experience that will put you on firmer footing for the next one.

You should take a positive view of the situation and expect the best. Your interviewer has a job to do and so do you. She or he has the task of selecting the best-qualified person for the job, and you have an obligation to do your best to meet her or his needs. There are no miracles in job interviewing. You and the competition are what you are—nothing more, nothing less. What you could do to prepare yourself for the opportunity has been done, and now it is time to relax and be a confident participant in the contest.

The chances are minuscule that anything devious is on the interviewer's mind. You are best advised to assume that you are entering a level playing field in which the interviewer honestly wants to see what you have to offer. You should assume that you will be interviewed in good faith, measured fairly, and ultimately judged on the merits.

Let your confidence in the fairness of the process and in your own outstanding qualifications show in your positive expectations as you participate in the interview. End the session thinking the best of everyone involved and mentally getting ready to move on to the next phase—accepting their offer of employment.

COMMUNICATING TECHNOLOGICAL AWARENESS

Candidates for most jobs, technical and otherwise, face the challenge of presenting themselves as being a good fit for the employer's technology environment. How they handle it depends on the position for which they are applying, their place on the technology continuum, and the actual situation.

If you are a non-technical person, your objective is to come across as someone familiar with workplace technology as a user. Whatever your field, technology surely serves it and you should understand the role of technology, be conversant in the jargon associated with it, and be able to demonstrate at least minimal skills in using it.

As you go up the management chain, expectations for the ratio of hands-on technological expertise to simple awareness change. The manager may not be expected to be a programmer, but it could be awkward if he were unable to perform routine operations using spreadsheet and word processing software. It might also raise eyebrows if she couldn't find her way around the Internet or use presentation software. Management candidates have to instill in the hiring committee confidence that they are aware of technology, can function intelligently with it, and know enough about it to hire and manage technical staff.

Technical people applying for positions on predominantly non-technical staffs have other problems to overcome. They need to come across as communicators who can relate to both worlds. People understand that they have to acquire someone with unique skills, but hiring committees react poorly to people who cannot relate to them on their own terms. They fear the "Data Nazi"—the technical staffer who somehow threatens to restrict and control the way they do business.

Your challenge as a technical-expert applicant is to show reasonable understanding of the business in which you will function. Convey your understanding that technology is just one more way to accomplish the overall mission of the organization. Lead with the caveat that you would have to be there a while before determining how appropriate such ideas might be, but relate how you see technology making the organization more productive.

SUMMARY CHECKLIST: DURING THE INTERVIEW

- It is time to impress your interviewer with honesty; job knowledge; a pleasing personality; and a believable, consistent pattern of interviewing behavior.

- Be a tactful but strong advocate of your own qualifications for the job.

- Expect to influence the interview's direction with the way you answer and ask questions.

- Transform yourself from an ink-and-paper resume image into a flesh-and-blood person.

- Understand that background checks are necessary because a significant number of job applications are exaggerated or untrue.

- Be enthusiastic about the interview and the opportunity.

- Recognize that you can affect your mental attitude, and use that knowledge to maintain a positive view of the interviewing situation.

- Make an effort to like and be liked in the interview process.

- Being courteous throughout the interview process can make you an attractive candidate.

- Expect to adapt to your interviewer's style and energy level.

- Minimize drinking and totally avoid smoking unless it is very clearly shown to be an acceptable practice where you are interviewing.

- Be prepared to accept different kinds of personalities at your interview.

- Sensibly use your knowledge of the company to sell yourself at the interview.

- Make learning more about the job an early priority in your interview so you can focus your presentation correctly.

- Identify the decision maker and direct your attention to satisfying his or her priorities.

- Hold discussion of your salary concerns until later, when a strong interest has developed in hiring you.

- Show interest in your interviewer.

- Learn the rules for dealing with interviewer questions, including reading the interview situation as it unfolds rather than concentrating blindly on your own performance.

- Be prepared for "behavioral interviewing," where you are asked to be more expansive in answering questions about your performance.
- Take time to think before you respond.
- Expect the difficult question and be ready for it.
- Recognize the motives behind the questions.
- Avoid negative comments about former employers and colleagues.
- Understand the applied psychology of job interviewing.
- Be alert to the messages sent by body language.
- Have positive expectations about your success during the interview.
- Communicate your awareness of workplace technology.

Internet Tip

If you want to try a "virtual interview" on the Internet, visit http://www.aboutwork.com/ace/virtual.html to complete an exercise called "Ace the Interview." For more help enter the keywords "virtual job interview" in your favorite search engine and follow the hyperlinks.

5

AFTER THE INTERVIEW

Your interview is just one more step along the way to getting hired—there is more to come. This chapter prepares you for what comes next—skillfully "closing the sale" after you have presented "the product." It covers four phases in the interview cycle: (1) leaving the interview, (2) evaluating the interview, (3) interview follow-up, and (4) concluding the interview process.

Leaving the Interview

You have a right to relax as you leave the interview, but not to stop thinking about or working on getting the job. There are important things still to be accomplished—mistakes to correct, favorable impressions to leave. Look at Figure 5 and orient yourself in the job interview cycle. Review the thumbnail sketch of what you are about to examine in detail and remind yourself of its importance in your goal of getting hired.

KEEPING YOUR STORY STRAIGHT

If you are in the midst of a comprehensive job search, you are probably juggling more than one interview and need to keep track of the facts and a multiple cast of characters. Few things are more damaging to your prospects of getting hired than a follow-up call or a thank-you note that confuses the facts. Either one of them betrays what no employer wants to hear—not only did she or he fail to leave an in-

GETTING THE INTERVIEW
- Finding a job
- Applying
- Networking
- Getting invited

PREPARING FOR THE INTERVIEW
- Researching the company
- Preparing personally
- Anticipating questions

APPEARING FOR THE INTERVIEW
- Reconnaissance
- Personal readiness
- Timing

DURING THE INTERVIEW
- Names and personalities
- Style and substance
- Satisfying agendas

LEAVING THE INTERVIEW
- Reading your audience
- Positive expectations
- Last impression

EVALUATING YOUR INTERVIEW
- Substantive match
- Personal chemistry
- Judging your chances

FOLLOWING UP AFTER YOUR INTERVIEW
- Thank you's
- Additional information
- More networking

CONCLUDING THE INTERVIEW PROCESS
- The offer
- Negotiating
- Accepting

You are still being evaluated and making judgments of your own as you leave the interview. As you rise, shake hands, thank your interviewer, and make your way out past the receptionist, subtle judgments continue to be made that could weigh heavily at decision time. This is when you express continuing interest. Leave with the last image being an upbeat, expectant, can-do person—and a firm handshake. Look for the best in your interviewer, but be alert to any signs of wrong or incomplete impressions that a follow-up might correct. Don't overstay your welcome, read the body language, and help your interviewer conclude the session gracefully.

Figure 5. Leaving the Interview.

delible impression on you, you are also talking with a rival firm. It is unforgivable for you to confuse someone with a competitor.

As soon as you clear the interview area—when you get to your car or settle into a cab—make a brief summary of names and events that will jog your memory in the future as the facts begin to fade. While it is possible to take notes during the interview, that can be awkward and distract you when you should be fully alert to what is going on. Save it for when you leave, but don't ignore the task after the high motivation that accompanies the interview session passes. You will need the particulars to impress your interviewers with thorough and accurate recall in your follow-up calls and correspondence.

THE EVALUATION GOES ON

The two-way process of evaluation is anything but over after the final handshake. Everyone involved continues in the evaluation process on some subtle level. The opinion of your interviewer is the most important, but everyone involved matters. When decision time comes, the hiring official looks for consensus. Everyone from his or her number two person to the receptionist will have some degree of influence. Remember that as you make your exit. Polite good-byes, thank you's, and gently applied personal charm are in your interest as you leave.

The way you handle your exit comments and actions varies with individual people. You express your continuing interest and appreciation for professional courtesies to your peers and seniors. Support staff get a heartfelt kind word for their help in making your travel arrangements, taking care of telephone messages, or whatever they did to make your visit a pleasant one. Everyone gets a polite, interested smile and "Thanks. I'll look forward to seeing you again." No one is left with any negative impression—"Where's my cab? I asked you to have one waiting when I came out of there!" You can't afford to have even the lowest-level eyes roll when your name gets mentioned during the decision-making phase.

Remember to say your good-byes in a style that is natural for you. This is no time to come on as a backslapper if you are a reserved type—just let the real you say, "Thanks. You made a difference in my interview day. I appreciate that and look forward to seeing you again." Such thoughtful small extensions of courtesy cost you nothing and can make a difference in the ultimate outcome of your interview.

LET IT END

Your interview is a two-way street right up to the end. Both you and the interviewer begin to signal when it is time to quit. Sometimes the end is dictated by the clock running out—another appointment is waiting, for example. More often, the two of you have said what there is to say—she or he has asked the questions, you have made your points, and the interview is complete.

One way to sour an otherwise good interview is by not knowing when to leave. The body language and verbal cues should signal that—looking at his or her watch, rearranging and closing your file, sitting back from his or her desk, making closing remarks. This is not the time to open new lines of inquiry or offer elaborate clarifications on points already made. Neither should you push for a decision that is not to be made at that point. You need to be ready to accept a gracious "Thanks for stopping by, I'll be getting back to you..." if that is how the session ends. All the better if your interviewer is clamoring to schedule you tomorrow with the big boss before someone else can steal you away, but don't rely on such a dramatic outcome. Express your appreciation, offer to cooperate in future efforts to clarify your qualifications, say that your interest in the job continues (if that is the case), and say good-bye.

FINAL BUSINESS

It is perfectly correct to ask what comes next or when a decision might be expected, if that information has not been volunteered. You have probably already been given instructions on reimbursement for your interviewing expenses. If not, take that up with personnel or your clerical point of contact the next day, not with the interviewer as you leave the session. Let the parting be professional.

CHANGE OF HEART

If you learn in the course of the interview that the position is not what you had in mind, you have an obligation to say so graciously as the interview ends. Sometimes the chemistry is wrong or the duties and level of responsibility are not up to your expectations. When that is the case, express your appreciation for the interview and then take yourself and the interviewer off the hook by withdrawing your name from further consideration. You can give it a positive twist by mentioning that you were impressed by the company and its people but that the particular position doesn't sound right for you at this time; if something comes up that the interviewer would consider more appropriate, you would welcome the opportunity to discuss it. That kind of ending leaves everyone feeling satisfied and ready to do business without unnecessary tension should future circumstances call for it.

Leaving Summary

- Avoid the temptation to ask how you did.

- Don't raise questions about salary or benefits.

- Ask what's next in the hiring cycle, suggest scheduling your next interview before leaving, but don't push for a hiring decision.

- Summarize the key requirements and link your attributes to them.

- Get the answers to any remaining questions you might have—briefly.

- Be prepared to accept an offer—contingent on terms to be negotiated later.

- Know who your interviewers were and their correct titles.

- Think and act positively, even if there were rough spots.

- Leave as you entered, with a confident handshake, a smile, and pleasantly enthusiastic about what is to come.

Evaluating Your Interview

You have survived the interview, made your way out of the building, and taken the requisite notes for future reference. Now it is time to evaluate how you did. As you settle into the drive home or get ready for a drink and two bags of airline peanuts, reflect on how it went. Be honest with yourself on these dimensions of your job interview:

- How did you do on the objective matters?
  - ✓ Did you measure up to their expectations?
  - ✓ Did they measure up to your expectations?
- What about subjective details?
  - ✓ Did your personalities mesh well?
  - ✓ Was the corporate culture to your liking?
- What is your gut feeling regarding your prospects?
  - ✓ Did you get the job?
  - ✓ Do you still want the job?

Figure 6 highlights the evaluation stage of job interviewing. Examine it as you prepare to learn more about this crucial step that brings you almost to the decision point in the hiring cycle.

LOOKING AT THE OPPORTUNITY OBJECTIVELY

Now that you have had your interview and discussed what the job consists of with the principals, you are in a better position to judge your fit for it. Look at it candidly from the following two perspectives.

DID YOU MEASURE UP TO THEIR EXPECTATIONS?

Put yourself in the place of the people who interviewed you. The interview has brought you closer to knowing what they really want. What do you think? Would you hire yourself if you were in the interviewers' position? You don't know exactly what they're thinking, but put yourself in their shoes and answer these questions:

- Did you have the qualifications, or was there something seriously missing from your training and experience?

- How was your fit on the seniority dimension? Were you right for this particular job, or would you be coming in either too "light" or too "heavy" to function well in it?

Work with these points as you recall specific questions and comments at the interview. Make a tentative judgment on whether you came out a winner from the employer's point of view. You don't have to force a definitive answer, but sometimes you find yourself clearly positioned at one or the other end of the continuum—a sure winner or a likely loser. Chances are you will rate yourself in the ambiguous middle that says you are still in the running and will just have to wait for the official decision.

DID THEY MEASURE UP TO YOUR EXPECTATIONS?

You have taken the trouble to apply, prepare, and interview. Momentum alone is pushing you to take a favorable view of the opportunity by this point in the hiring cycle. But is it really warranted? How do you feel about the job now? Before you rush headlong into a questionable move, objectively think through these points:

- Will this job challenge your abilities and ambition, or is it more of what you already have? Less than what you want?

GETTING THE INTERVIEW
- Finding a job
- Applying
- Networking
- Getting invited

PREPARING FOR THE INTERVIEW
- Researching the company
- Preparing personally
- Anticipating questions

APPEARING FOR THE INTERVIEW
- Reconnaissance
- Personal readiness
- Timing

DURING THE INTERVIEW
- Names and personalities
- Style and substance
- Satisfying agendas

LEAVING THE INTERVIEW
- Reading your audience
- Positive expectations
- Last impression

EVALUATING YOUR INTERVIEW
- Substantive match
- Personal chemistry
- Judging your chances

You are out of the interview and on your way home. It is time for an honest look at how you did—and what you now think of the opportunity you are seeking. First you examine the substantive things and determine whether you fill the bill and vice versa. Next you make judgments of whether you clicked with the personalities involved, how well the corporate culture seemed to fit your style and values. Being both positive and candid with yourself, assess your chances of getting the job—and whether you still want it.

FOLLOWING UP AFTER YOUR INTERVIEW
- Thank you's
- Additional information
- More networking

CONCLUDING THE INTERVIEW PROCESS
- The offer
- Negotiating
- Accepting

Figure 6. Evaluating Your Interview.

- What does it do for your career? Is this position going to place you on the bottom rung of an opportunity ladder with a fast track to the top, or is it just an insignificant step up with nowhere in particular to go next?

You need candid answers to these questions, and you are the only person to provide them. This is no time to become negative about the opportunity, but respect your gut feelings if the job doesn't feel right in the reality of your evaluation.

LOOKING AT THE OPPORTUNITY SUBJECTIVELY

You have now met some of the people you will be working with, and you are in a better position to judge the chemistry. How do you feel about your potential colleagues and working relationships?

WERE THE PERSONALITIES COMPATIBLE?

This is the time for you to be totally honest with yourself. If you were a fish out of water during the interview and plant tour, now is the time to acknowledge it—not six months after taking the job when you find yourself isolated, unhappy, and in the midst of people whose values and workstyle you do not share. Think about it in the context of these questions:

- How was the chemistry and the comfort level?
- Were you at ease with your interviewers, or were you psychologically out of step all day?
- Was the humor your kind of humor, or was it nonexistent?
- Did they seem like bright, motivated people?
- Did you find a worthy mental sparring partner for the future?
- Were these people interesting?
- Were the energy levels within range of your own?
- Any troubling signs on the basic values? Honesty? Social consciousness? Environmental awareness? Fiscal responsibility? Basic morality?

WHAT ABOUT THE CORPORATE CULTURE?

It matters how you feel about the people you will be working with, but it is also important that you are comfortable with the feel and the style of the organization you are joining. Here are a few things to consider:

- Is this a fitness-oriented group that is not to your taste?

- Is it a highly social group after hours that doesn't suit you?

- Is it a smoking environment?

- Is the form of address too casual between every layer of the organization?

- Is the energy level of the office too frantic for you?

- Do you share the organization's social and ethical values?

- Are you comfortable with the dress code?

- Are you comfortable with formal business hours and time accounting procedures?

- Is the business travel policy something with which you can live?

These are the kinds of corporate culture considerations that you should evaluate as you decide how to proceed. The job can be quite attractive but the atmosphere in which you have to function, the opposite. Mismatches of personal and corporate style can affect your happiness and future success in an organization. Without overemphasizing peripheral considerations, don't disregard their importance as you evaluate your prospects and how you will respond when the job offer comes.

You have to use discretion in gathering this kind of information. Do it informally in your research and with the help of people in your network. You don't want to leave a negative impression by asking some of these things directly. Instead, you should look for opportunities to observe and seek subtle clarifications as you deal with the more routine questions of your interview.

FEELINGS ABOUT YOUR PROSPECTS

As you put your objective and subjective impressions about the interview together, you form an impression of what your chances are for getting the job. You can be wrong, but it usually is not hard to separate the two extremes—you ran especially strong, or weak. If your performance is in the middle range, it is difficult to judge. You can explore your prospects on the important dimensions that follow.

DID YOU GET THE JOB?

There are times when you leave the interview with the distinct impression that it's all over—something didn't ring true, and you have been given the polite boot out the door, never to return. The opposite outcome is easier to judge and a far more comfortable feeling. Like the insider encouraged with winks and nods, the successful interviewee receives signals—often unmistakable.

Reading the Signs of How Well You Did

- What was the tone as you left the interview—formal and distant? Or relaxed and "familial"?

- Were there anxious questions about your availability? Or best wishes for success in your job search?

- Was it, "I want you to call me tomorrow afternoon about a few things we need to work out" or, "I'll be in touch in a few weeks after the interviews are complete"?

- Were you advised in confidence, "We have a few more people we have to see, but frankly, I'd like you to start tomorrow; call me before you accept anything else" or, "You are one of seven candidates we are considering for the position; the selection committee will advise you of your status in two weeks"?

Many times the cues are less obvious, but they can all tell you a lot that the interviewer would never formally reveal. Listen for indicators as you leave the interview and in the calls and letters that follow. You should not get terribly discouraged if the winks and nods are not thrown your way—many hirings are simply done by the book, with no relief from the "by the numbers" ritual. You can come out of the most uncomfortable interview a winner.

DO YOU STILL WANT THE JOB?

Momentum can be dangerous. It can lead you into a career move you would never make if you considered it calmly. The evaluation stage of the interview cycle is where you owe yourself some honest answers, even if they are disrupting. It is your career, and you are the person who has to function in the job every day. It is time for you to take a mental cold shower and candidly answer some questions.

Is This the Job You Really Want?

- Is it the opportunity you pictured?

- Are they the kind of colleagues you'll thrive working with?

- Is the corporate culture one in which you'll be comfortable?

- Do you still feel confident that you have what it takes to do the job and meet the company's expectations?

- Are things that bad where you are now?

You need to accomplish this personal evaluation of your job interview before you implement the next step: follow-up. After the evaluation phase, you are ready to focus on an effective follow-up that reinforces the interview and sets the stage for hiring. Clear away your doubts and reaffirm your motivation to get the job before you go further; commitment or the lack of it shows, and it can play a significant role in your final rating by those who will make the hiring decision.

Evaluation Summary

- Whom have I met? What do they do? What do I think of them?
- What have I learned about the job that I didn't know before?
- Where would I begin—first projects, principal challenges?
- Can I handle the job?
- Will the job challenge and reward me?
- What were my weak points in the interview? Can I overcome them?
- What can I expect next in the hiring cycle?
- How did interview really end? Positively? Brush-off?
- Do I really want this job?

Interview Follow-up

Now you must strengthen your case for turning the interview into a job offer. You want to say thanks and let the interviewer know that you (1) left the session feeling good about the job, and (2) that you still have a strong interest in it. Here are the topics you want to consider in planning your follow-up:

- Reinforce the good impressions you made.
- Perform any necessary damage control.
- Provide additional information that would be helpful.
- Activate your network for both feedback and influence.
- Prepare for any subsequent interviews.

Before going on to the follow-up procedures, look at Figure 7 to get your bearings as you get ready to conclude the interviewing cycle successfully. Scan where you've been and where you still have to go to avoid getting bogged down in already

GETTING THE INTERVIEW
- Finding a job
- Applying
- Networking
- Getting invited

PREPARING FOR THE INTERVIEW
- Researching the company
- Preparing personally
- Anticipating questions

APPEARING FOR THE INTERVIEW
- Reconnaissance
- Personal readiness
- Timing

DURING THE INTERVIEW
- Names and personalities
- Style and substance
- Satisfying agendas

LEAVING THE INTERVIEW
- Reading your audience
- Positive expectations
- Last impression

EVALUATING YOUR INTERVIEW
- Substantive match
- Personal chemistry
- Judging your chances

FOLLOWING UP AFTER YOUR INTERVIEW
- Thank you's
- Additional information
- More networking

CONCLUDING THE INTERVIEW PROCESS
- The offer
- Negotiating
- Accepting

Your interview is history, and you've made your initial judgment on how you did. Now it's time for reinforcing the good impressions you made, damage control (if there were rough spots), filling any information gaps that might make your case stronger, and bringing to bear any influence you might have within the organization. This is a delicate phase where you must avoid pushing too hard or letting the opportunity slip away by doing too little. Use your network to get objective impressions of where you stand and what the best approach would now be. Prepare for any follow-up interviews.

Figure 7. Following Up After Your Interview.

completed tasks or jumping too quickly into things such as salary negotiations that are best left for last. You've come a long way and need to comprehend the efforts that now have you poised on the brink of a successful job offer. Everything is coming together as planned. Finish the process now with an outstanding follow-up effort.

REINFORCING THE GOOD IMPRESSIONS

Let's assume you walked out of the interview a winner. Everyone liked you, and it showed. Just as important, you liked them—now let *that* show in a tasteful, professional way.

SAYING THANK YOU

You have one perfectly good excuse to reestablish contact after your job interview—and that is to express your appreciation. No one can fault you for saying thanks in writing, and it is an opportunity to say much more. E-mail is an ideal medium for the post-interview note of thanks. It is at once appropriately prompt, informal, and businesslike. While you don't want to overdo a good thing, your letter of appreciation for the job interview can also be the occasion you need to make a few points.

Points to Make in Your Letter of Appreciation

- The job was even more exciting than you imagined it would be. Then mention a point or two to validate your statement and keep it from sounding like ingenuous postinterview fluff.

- You felt quite comfortable with the staff and were pleased to learn that you share common professional interests, backgrounds, and aspirations (be careful in spelling out other people's aspirations—you might get someone in trouble).

- You are available for subsequent interviews or inquiries should either become necessary.

- You want the job.

CALLING THE INTERVIEWER

Use your judgment to determine whether an e-mail or a letter of appreciation is sufficient or if a telephone call is also in order. It isn't good to appear overly anxious, and the letter is probably enough, unless you have an existing relationship with the interviewer that eases the way for a more personal expression of gratitude. Another approach is to let some time pass, make a brief call to say thanks, reaffirm interest, and check on the status of the hiring. If your call is not returned, don't push the issue. Understand that formal hiring procedures are being followed and you can expect notification when everyone receives it.

When you have to decide about another job offer, you have nothing to lose by calling, waiting a reasonable amount of time for it to be returned, then calling again, this time leaving the message that you need to know your status in order to make another employment decision. Chances are you will be told that no decision can be reached at that point, but it is worth inquiring just in case they are on the verge of an offer you can't refuse.

DAMAGE CONTROL

You sometimes need to undo a mistaken impression that could not be resolved to your satisfaction during the interview. A deliberately difficult question may have baited you into a response that you still don't feel right about. You have to decide whether it was intended to force the awkward moment you experienced, or something more. If it was the latter, you can't go wrong sending a brief, businesslike letter clarifying your position.

Remember that the "rules of damage control" include a healthy respect for letting sleeping dogs lie. You might be wise not to reopen an awkward moment or amplify genuine differences with the interviewer. Choose your instances for controlling damage carefully, and take initiatives only when you have clearly left behind a situation that can be improved by further attention. When in doubt, leave it alone.

Once you are convinced that the wrong message was conveyed and you have the ability to correct it, set the record straight. Properly done, damage control can turn an interview around for you by clarifying the matter and showing your skill in handling a sensitive situation. It can make you stand out favorably in the crowd and increase your odds of getting the job.

SENDING ADDITIONAL INFORMATION

Your interviewer sometimes reveals a strong interest or discloses a problem that he or she would dearly like to solve. If you have knowledge of the topic, go ahead and share it conversationally during the interview—but you can do more. Perhaps you have seen an article on the subject. When you get home, send a copy to the interviewer with a business card or a short "for your information" note attached. It is a thoughtful, understated way to show interest in a person who can help you. You position yourself as a colleague by this kind of exchange, and it can enhance your image and make you memorable at decision time. Other things being equal, such gestures can make a difference.

Such an approach gives you a chance to provide additional information in the form of straightforward data whose usefulness became apparent to you during the interview. Occasionally after you leave an interview you see something that makes just the point on which you and your interviewer so strongly agreed. Forward it with your card and a brief note resurrecting the moment, saying you enjoyed the exchange of views and wishing him or her success in hiring the right person. It can't hurt and might become the tie-breaking personal touch that gets you the job.

ACTIVATING YOUR NETWORK

After your interview, look for feedback from anyone you know who has an ear to the hiring environment. The more direct the source the better, but don't overlook anyone who can tell you what kind of impression you made. At this point, make the connections and let the information flow from wherever it might. Make the qualitative judgments later. Get as many views from independent sources as you can.

Consistency is one way to confirm the accuracy of what you are being told. Use the information as another source for judging where you stand and what you might do to improve your chances. The quality of this kind of feedback varies widely, so leave room for personal judgment before taking it too seriously. Unless the source is someone you personally know and trust, sift the information carefully, and use it only in combination with other indicators that point to similar conclusions.

A second way for you to use your network following the interview is to bring third-party influence to bear. You have to do this sparingly and with considerable care, but it can be a useful technique. If you know people who are respected by the hiring organization, this is the time for them to check discreetly on your status. Since it is obvious that they want to see you hired, finesse is needed. A skillful politician can give your prospects new life with the right touch; a clumsy one can hurt you. You are the person best able to judge the potential for help or harm—be cautious, but don't hesitate to use networking for influence as well as information when warranted. Here is a final summary of things you want to accomplish in your follow-up phase:

Interview Follow-up Summary

- Show your enthusiasm for the job.
- Demonstrate your understanding of the requirements.
- Summarize your competence for the job.
- Indicate that you want the job.
- Tell how you can contribute—be specific to the first project, if possible.
- Show that you listened by recapping a point the interviewer made (attribute it to him or her—"You suggested that...and I believe...").

- Be impressed with what you saw and whom you met—mention names.

- Say you're looking forward to whatever comes next—more interviews, an offer.

- Say thanks for the courtesies extended.

- Touch all bases—a letter to the most important managerial interviewer, copies to others with personal notes attached.

- One page is all it should take—be brief.

- Act now—go home and get your letter in the mail in time to affect the hiring process and revive your favorable image as decisions are being made.

- Unless you've been asked to call, wait a week before deciding that a telephone follow-up is necessary.

- Be prepared to exploit any turndown into more job leads.

GETTING READY FOR ANOTHER INTERVIEW

You may have a single interview or a series of them. If the one you just completed is the first of several, you need to go back to the earlier chapters on preparing for, appearing at, and performing during your interview. This is especially true if your subsequent interviews are to be of a different kind. For example, you may have passed an initial screening interview with the human resources officer coordinating the hiring and are about to face a selection interview with the department head who will hire you. You might also be facing a group interview where your ability to function with others is to be tested, or a panel interview in which you will be formally interviewed by several people. Do what you can to determine the nature of your next interview and use the preceding chapters and the information gained in the interview just ended to prepare for the next one.

Concluding the Interview Process

Everything you have done so far was to achieve one thing: an offer of employment. You found the job, applied for it successfully, prepared for the interviews, and passed them with flying colors. Now it is time to wrap it all up with the kind of terms that satisfy both you and your new employer. Here are the final steps in your job search cycle:

- receiving the offer of employment;
- deciding whether to pursue the offer;

- negotiating salary and terms of employment;
- getting the offer in writing;
- formally accepting the position; and
- notifying your present employer.

For the last time, see where you stand on the hiring continuum by looking at Figure 8. It shows you ready to conclude the job search in a way that leaves nothing in doubt. Too often in the euphoria of the offer, you let your disciplined approach lapse and settle for exactly what is offered. Sometimes you have no choice if it is a take-it-or-leave-it proposition. Some companies fill standard positions and offer uniform benefits with no room for negotiation, but usually there is something negotiable. While you certainly don't want to torpedo the deal by becoming unreasonable at this late hour in the hiring, there is nothing wrong with pausing to clarify the terms. In the process you can be sure of what you are getting and often improve some aspect of the offer.

THE OFFER OF EMPLOYMENT

Generally you will receive a congratulatory telephone call that constitutes an offer of employment and carries with it a presumption of on-the-spot acceptance. If the offer is to your liking, then by all means accept. You are the person in the best position to judge whether you have any leverage at this point. For example, your network may have informed you that it was a close decision with you getting the nod, but if you hesitate, the number two is a perfectly satisfactory choice. If that is the case, you are in no position to delay—take the job if you want it. On the other hand, your sources may have revealed that you were the only acceptable candidate or the strong first choice. In that situation you can probably accept conditionally using wording like this: "Thank you for the offer, Mr. Jones, everything sounds about right to me. Let's consider it a deal contingent on formally spelling out the fine points. When could we go over the remaining details?" Unless the offer is really out of line or you have totally lost interest in the position, it is worth seeing what can be worked out.

DECIDING ON WHETHER TO PURSUE THE OFFER

You have bought time with your contingency acceptance. Now you have to examine the offer calmly and decide whether it is attractive enough to pursue. The choice before you should not be a surprise, and the main points of comparison among the position offered, your present job, and other realistic opportunities call for little more than an informal review in your own mind. With that concluded, it is time to get on with the negotiations.

GETTING THE INTERVIEW
- Finding a job
- Applying
- Networking
- Getting invited

PREPARING FOR THE INTERVIEW
- Researching the company
- Preparing personally
- Anticipating questions

APPEARING FOR THE INTERVIEW
- Reconnaissance
- Personal readiness
- Timing

DURING THE INTERVIEW
- Names and personalities
- Style and substance
- Satisfying agendas

LEAVING THE INTERVIEW
- Reading your audience
- Positive expectations
- Last impression

EVALUATING YOUR INTERVIEW
- Substantive match
- Personal chemistry
- Judging your chances

FOLLOWING UP AFTER YOUR INTERVIEW
- Thank you's
- Additional information
- More networking

CONCLUDING THE INTERVIEW PROCESS
- The offer
- Negotiating
- Accepting

Your follow-up is complete. Everyone with influence in your network has spoken on your behalf and given you his or her impression of where you stand. You've answered all the questions, and an offer has been made. Now is the time to examine the compensation and benefits package in detail and see if it can be improved upon. This is also when your duties, authority, and place in the organization are defined. At this stage you are someone the employer wants and will try to accommodate.

Figure 8. Concluding the Interview Process.

NEGOTIATING SALARY AND TERMS OF EMPLOYMENT

Whether you are dealing face-to-face, over the telephone, or through the good offices of a third party such as an executive recruiter, the next phase requires realism and sensitivity. For most people who change jobs, the expected salary increase is 10 to 15 percent. If you are really in demand or grossly underpaid at present, it might be possible to make that 20 to 25 percent. Expect the employer to start with the lower figure. Know your market value and degree of attractiveness to other employers before coming back with your expectations. If you are working with a recruiter, he or she should be able to advise you on the realities of your situation and what the company will probably do. Make your expectations known in a professional way, have some rational basis for them (such as a reasonable increase over current salary plus next expected raise in your present position), and see what happens. You are putting the offer at risk in any negotiating situation. The employer can always take offense and withdraw the offer, but you can usually have a reasonable discussion that leaves room for compromise. Sometimes nonsalary items can sweeten the deal—more paid leave, time off for consulting, a stock option or a company car, a club membership. The possibilities are endless, and the trick to getting what you can is asking and making a plausible case for both the increased value you are placing on yourself and your worth to the company. You have to keep the two in balance to be successful in your negotiations. Here is how you want to go about conducting the negotiations.

Guidelines for Negotiating

- *Figure out what you are worth in the marketplace* by checking others in similar positions, those above and below you, government statistics, professional publications containing salary surveys, executive recruiters, and the want ads (especially the national ones).

> **Internet Tip**
>
> Salaries can be checked on the Internet. Try sites like http://www.dbm.com/jobguide/salary.html and http://jobsmart.org/tools/salary/sal-prof.htm/. You can also explore professional association and publication web pages in your specialty by entering their names in search engines or by calling their national offices to request URL's.

- *Determine whether you have room to negotiate* by finding out (if you can) how badly the company wants you and how many others are waiting to accept if you prove difficult. If you are ever in a position to affect your future earnings, this is it. Find out, and act accordingly.

- *Avoid settling for a percentage kicker to your present salary* by taking the attitude that your present compensation should not be the sole basis for determining your future salary, be as evasive as you can about disclosing current earnings (make them ask twice, give a range, include the value of your perks and benefits, and say that your salary has increased every year), try to steer the negotiations to what similar positions pay at the new company, but never refuse outright to give a truthful figure if pressed (it can always be verified, and you want to be able to defend your answer).

- *Test your expectations* by mentioning your desire to work for a company that will pay you what you are worth and not just place you on a salary schedule. Ask if they are in a position to do that, and if they are, suggest that it begin now by establishing your starting salary on your real value to them, not your past earnings or some arbitrary scale and step.

- *Avoid the "name a figure" trap* by recapping the responsibilities you see yourself having in a flattering way, then turn the question back by asking: "What did you expect to pay for someone who could handle all of that as well as I will be able to?" "What range did you have in mind?" "I've assumed from the beginning that you'd make me a fair offer—what do you have in mind?" Keep the focus on the responsibilities and remind them of their conclusion that you have what it takes to meet them.

- *Work the "ranges"* by defining a new one that is anchored in what they name but exceeds the limit. If they say $52,500 to $57,500, come back with the positive statement that you are both in the same ball park and express the hope that they have some flexibility on the up side—what you had in mind was a $55,000 to $60,000 range, with a midpoint starting salary. That would put you at the top of the scale they offered and give you growing room.

- *Don't bring on a "sorry, but we can't afford you" response* by staying away from absolutes. You can always talk in ranges that don't exceed theirs; you can always negotiate down.

- *Know what you are going to be worth in the future* by being aware of the compensation of people in the next few ranges. It will put you in a good position to respond intelligently to future expectation questions. Show that you are being realistic today, but know the progression expected for successful people in your industry.

- *Make one last try* by being very professional and businesslike but countering their offer with something like: "We are so close to agreement already, my career plans have projected just a little bit more at this stage—surely we have room for some final adjustments here?" Back off if they effectively say take it or leave it, but it is worth a polite final push.

- *If the offer really is too low, stay positive* by saying how complimented you are by their interest in you, how impressed you are by the situation and challenges outlined, how confident you are of succeeding and making a contribution—if only their initial offer could be improved. See if that brings a renewed effort to find a solution or a take-it-or-leave-it response.

- *Offer some alternatives* by suggesting that if you are exceeding the range, perhaps the position could be reclassified and you might be started near the bottom of the next range. Suggest starting where they must classify you, but with a hiring bonus and insured promotion at the end of a given time period if your work is satisfactory. While entry ranges are often sacred, bonus and promotion flexibility can sometimes compensate.

- *Price the perks* by seeing what might be made available to you in noncash compensation—paid memberships, medical and life insurance, automobile-related expenses, investment options, etc. Salary is not the only way to get paid, and every useful thing that can be provided directly is a dollar of direct compensation not spent. Dental, vision, and legal insurance are add-ons you might consider valuable, as are childcare allowances, profit sharing, paid days off for consulting, financial and tax planning assistance, and termination pay.

A WRITTEN OFFER OF EMPLOYMENT

Your next step is another contingency. Shake hands. Do whatever good-faith things are necessary to clinch the deal, and orally summarize your understanding of the terms but ask that they be put in writing before you resign your present position or they announce your acquisition. Just as good fences make good neighbors, so letters of understanding, if not formal employment contracts, make for good workplace relationships. Ask for the terms to be summarized in a letter signed by someone in authority, secure any clarifications and corrections that are necessary, then accept the terms with a letter of your own.

NOTIFYING YOUR PRESENT EMPLOYER

Only after you have a written offer of employment that is satisfactory to you should you prepare your letter of resignation and present it to your current employer. There are many instances where your departure is no surprise and your efforts to grow professionally have been fully and openly supported; that makes it easy. Other situations are less comfortable, and your resignation will be an awkward moment. Decide two things before making your move:

- *Your decision is irrevocable*—nothing the employer says is going to change your mind.

- *You will not be drawn into any rancor or bad feelings*—you will leave with positive feelings regardless of the possibility of a negative reaction when you resign.

There were valid career reasons for considering a change when you decided to seek another position, and they are equally true the day you resign. Faced with a valuable person's resignation, some employers will make what is known in recruiting circles as a "counteroffer/buyback." That is, they will offer you a raise that is good enough to keep you from leaving. Don't take it. Research shows that most people who do are not around for the long term. You have compromised your security by threatening to leave once, and they expect you to do it again. The usual objective of the counteroffer is to buy them time to replace you. Every such offer may not be so sinister, but the general truth of the matter is that once you have decided to move on, do it and don't look back.

You do owe your employer reasonable notice and an offer to cooperate in training your replacement, whenever he or she comes on board. It is in everyone's best interest to make your parting a positive experience. Express your gratitude for the opportunities you have enjoyed. Offer to be of any assistance you can be in the transition. Speak well of the company in the future. As you learned earlier in the hiring cycle, there is no room in the employment marketplace for bashing your previous employer.

SUMMARY CHECKLIST: AFTER THE INTERVIEW

- When you leave the interview, take notes and keep track of the facts and personalities involved.

- Realize that your evaluation continues as you leave the interview; continue to leave favorable impressions on your way out.

- Be sensitive to when the interviewer wants to conclude the session, and help him or her reach a gracious ending point.

- Limit your parting questions to a brief expression of continuing interest in what comes next; take care of housekeeping tasks such as travel reimbursements later.

- Bow out graciously and positively if you determine that the position is not for you.

- Be positive but objective in assessing how you did.

- Be candid with yourself about how much you want the job now that you know more about it.

- Realistically try to rate your chances of receiving an offer.

- Be ready to deal with an offer.

- Realize that your compensation package is worth negotiating, and know how to handle the process without turning the employer off.

- Always get the offer in writing before resigning from your present job; accept orally contingent on a written offer.

- Resign with dignity—express your appreciation for the opportunity just passed, give adequate notice, and offer to cooperate in the transition.

PART

II

MORE INTERVIEW STRATEGIES

6 TECHNOLOGY AND THE INTERVIEW

You might encounter electronic technology, and maybe even a little pseudoscience, in the course of your job interview. This is especially true in large corporations and government agencies. Some of it will be straightforward attempts to make communication between you and the interviewer easier—satellites, videotapes, and computers. In other cases, computers linked to various databases will verify the correctness of claims you made on your resume and application. Still other devices and materials try to measure everything from how honest you are to how well you might perform certain tasks or get along with people. As debates continue in professional and regulatory circles about the accuracy and fairness of some of these measures, you need to be aware of them and how your hiring might be affected. This chapter will discuss:

- computer-based background checking;
- computer-assisted interviewing;
- satellite interviewing;
- videotaped interviewing;
- polygraph (lie detector) testing;
- psychological and aptitude testing;
- handwriting analysis; and
- physiological testing.

Looking at the list, you can see that things such as computer-based background checking are commonplace. If you ever had a driver's license, a credit card, subscribed to a magazine, had a criminal conviction, joined the military, or held a job, you are in someone's electronic database. While satellite, videotaped, and computer-assisted interviewing are rare, knowing about them can keep you from being surprised and performing badly if they are used. Your main concerns for abuse by an employer are handwriting analysis and the three testing procedures—sometimes questionable approaches that can screen you out of a job. This chapter will tell you about these practices and the issues surrounding them in the belief that familiarity in itself is effective preparation for dealing with them. You will also find the latest legal and regulatory information regarding them discussed in Chapter 8, "Interviewing and the Law."

Computer-Based Background Checking

One of your first encounters with technology in hiring may be the ordinary credit check. What used to be a secret, mysterious process was opened to public view after it became controversial when its mistakes hurt people. Now credit history reporting is so accessible that you can subscribe to your own report. If you are a credit card holder, you have probably been asked to "subscribe" to your own credit report—one way to protect yourself from errors that can creep into your file. Another consumer protection added by the regulators in recent years is that you must be given the name of any credit reporting agency that furnishes a negative report on you. You are entitled to a free copy of the damaging report and a chance to challenge the errors.

While the way you handle your personal finances is of interest to employers, some go further and check the extensive personal histories that are available on you. Depending on the employer, you might have anything checked from arrest records to the demographic profile of your zip code—it is all a matter of record somewhere. Although access to your personal files is theoretically limited, a determined investigator can learn everything about you, from your spending habits to your personal tastes, by working with companies who interpret the many electronic "audit trails" you leave behind in the process of modern living. Former landlords, neighbors, employers, and colleagues are only a telephone call away from anyone who wants to check you out. Any investigator who will devote a few hours to calling the most obvious sources can ask what they know, whom they suggest calling for further information, and quickly end up with a revealing picture of your lifestyle and character.

Not all of these "Big Brother" approaches are threats to your job interview. Some of the sources can actually be helpful to you, since they verify your claims.

But you need to appreciate how naïve it would be to misrepresent yourself in an employment marketplace that has access to so much information.

While the scope of any investigation depends on the nature of the position you are pursuing, how much trouble the employer will likely go to, or the kinds of access he or she will have, you should assume a thorough investigation and keep your application, resume, and interview responses scrupulously honest. Your application to the Central Intelligence Agency is obviously going to invite more scrutiny than a marketing position with a consumer services company, but be prepared for any employer's interest in verifying your good character, responsible lifestyle, and honesty about your claims to education and experience.

Computer-Assisted Interviewing

A standard complaint you hear about job interviewing is that the interviewers are not trained to be objective. They have a tendency to hire people they like—people with *their* characteristics—for jobs not at all like the one they hold. The result is an unsatisfactory match of candidate and position.

Companies are trying to solve the problem by making your interview more objective. Trained interviewers are asking questions that are more controlled, demanding, wide-ranging, and systematic than they would be in a natural, conversational interview. The structured interview is popular among those who value objectivity.

The ultimate in objective preemployment screening is the computer-assisted job interview, where a computer is programmed to ask you the questions; your touchscreen responses are digitized, and your body language is recorded on videotape. All of it is analyzed later by a human resources specialist who may have no personal interaction with you.

Theoretically, such an approach reduces the potential for an interviewer identifying with you personally and losing his or her objectivity. Critics claim that the most revealing thing about the approach is that it tells the applicant he or she is interviewing with an impersonal company with a cold corporate culture.

Computer-assisted interviewing can, of course, have its place without dehumanizing the hiring process. It might prove to be an efficient and reliable way for covering truly routine screening questions. Done right, that can leave more time and energy for meaningful interaction between you and the interviewer and ensure a better-informed hiring for each of you. Others argue that it is through the seemingly routine questions that you and your interviewer reveal yourselves enough to judge accurately your fit for the job and the people with whom you would be working.

Some job-related testing is also done using computers. You might be asked to complete a personality or a skills test sitting at a computer console. This is done by computer for administrative convenience, not to test your computer skills. Don't be surprised, though, if you are asked to use a computer terminal to enter data and respond to questions during an interview. It is a chance to verify basic computer literacy, and you might encounter this job requirement at almost any position level today. You should prepare for that possibility by learning the basics of operating a personal computer. By doing so you eliminate one more potential surprise at interview time and gain a useful skill that can be mentioned even if you are not asked to demonstrate it. Personal computer rental centers are everywhere, so it isn't necessary to purchase one to learn the basics—preparing your resume and job search correspondence is a good excuse for conquering the PC.

Satellite Interviewing

Your interview can be an expensive proposition for an employer if travel is involved. The solution for an increasing number of employers is using satellite technology to do the job—or part of it. As a job candidate interviewing with a distant company, you might be asked to take part in what amounts to an "individual videoconference"—a satellite-linked job interview. More colleges and companies have the capability, and the technique may soon be widely available through commercial placement services in major cities.

Freeze-frame videotelephones have been available for years. They are a novelty item and offer little in the way of real visual interaction between you and the person on the other end of the line. But the technology improved dramatically and it is now possible truly to interact during a telephone conversation.

Many companies and universities see satellite-based interviewing mainly as an extension of essential in-person campus recruiting sessions. They like the idea that others at the company can have follow-up interviews with you—after your initial talk with their campus recruiter—without paying for additional trips.

If you are situated off the beaten path, your chances of getting an interview of any kind improve when the cost of travel is reduced by satellite-based interviewing. College placement officers are aware of how much more competitive their graduates become with access to satellite interviewing, and they are encouraging wider use of the technology.

While your chances of being interviewed by satellite are still slight, at least twenty-five universities use the technology, and the prospects for growth are good. You are most apt to encounter it as a student in a college that has linked itself to technology-oriented companies. In the future you can look forward to the possibility of finding commercial satellite-based placement offices located throughout the country and catering to all kinds of candidates and employers.

Internet Tip

To see an example of Internet job interviewing, go to http://iamag.com/ infoage/virtual.htm and explore "CU-SeeMe" interviewing. If the URL changes, try "CU-SeeMe" or "virtual job interviewing" on your search engine.

Videotaped Interviewing

You can videotape your resume or a mock interview and have a greater impact on employers who would otherwise not have gotten beyond your paper resume—the ones who would not have interviewed you personally. While videotape technology can be useful in your job search, you need to be cautious in dealing with companies selling the service.

Start by checking the reputation of the videotaped resume service. Some video companies have excellent connections with personnel departments who are anxious to review what they produce, but others are like video dating services that make their money taping you and don't do much beyond that point. You want to avoid paying for a glamorous and costly approach to marketing yourself that will have little real impact. Ask for references from both individual clients and employers who use the service. You should be able to verify that major employers in your field are receptive to what you are preparing for them before investing your money.

Opinions vary on the potential value of your video resume. Some employers and candidates welcome the technology as a way to get beyond the paper resume without incurring the cost of an in-person interview. Others share the view of Brian Dumaine, whose *Fortune* magazine article discounted them as fluff. His advice to employers?

Start by tossing gimmicky resumes into the circular file—the job seeker has probably already submitted hundreds of regular resumes to no avail. In particular, do not be taken in by the latest craze in job hunting: the video resume. Here a job applicant makes his pitch on a video tape, then sends it out to potential employers. Some job seekers spend up to $300 on professional scripts and coaching to make themselves look better on tape than they ever would on the job. Unless you're looking for a model or an actor, skip the five or ten minutes it takes to look over a video resume.

Mr. Dumaine is more negative than most in his views. Your best bet is to be aware that opinions like his exist and verify that the employers you are approaching don't share his skepticism before you invest.

Do-it-yourself efforts offer an alternative to the expensive video resume and interviewing companies, but you risk looking like an amateur unless you are talented and have good equipment. You might also consider having your own script taped at a professional studio and doing your own distribution. The best combination of value, impact, and economy will vary with your circumstances.

Another approach to video interviewing that you might encounter is illustrated by a Florida firm that works directly for corporate clients that have already gone through the regular interview advertising and screening processes. These companies contract to have you videotaped, according to Paul Brown, writing in *INC.* magazine, when they have identified a dozen or so finalists whom they next want to see. You are invited to one of twenty-four videotaping offices around the country, where you and your competition are asked the same questions, in the same order, and the resulting tapes represent each of you in the next round of screening at the company's home offices.

Your video interview can contribute a lot to the evaluation process if the employer is receptive to using it. What you and the employer gain is animation and a degree of humanization that your paper resume doesn't have. What your video still lacks is the interactive exchange of a face-to-face or satellite interview—the priceless follow-up questions and elaboration are missing. While there is always the chance that a weak video performance will deny you an in-person interview you might have gotten without it, the chance is generally worth taking. Use your video option whenever it promises to advance you beyond the paper resume stage. Of course, if you have the option of going directly for an in-person session, skip the videotape and go for the real thing. Video resumes and mock interviews, desirable as they may be under many circumstances, are no substitute for one-to-one interactive interviewing.

Polygraph (Lie Detector) Testing

Unless you are a candidate for a security-related government job or plan to work in particularly sensitive areas of the commercial sector, polygraph testing is now prohibited by federal law. Employers are not allowed to use it except in special situations. Chapter 8, "Interviewing and the Law," discusses the legal and regulatory aspects of polygraph use and tells you what to do if you are confronted with inappropriate electronic testing.

Psychological and Aptitude Testing

PSYCHOLOGICAL TESTS

"Psychological testing" is a broad term used to describe techniques that are intended to measure human behavior in reasonably systematic ways. Different versions of it are used by employers who try to figure out everything from your intelligence to your honesty. In the course of an employment interview cycle you might be asked to respond to written questions, manipulate objects, perform role-playing tasks with other people, or have an interview with a psychologist to reveal job-relevant things about your personality and abilities. The likelihood for psychological testing has increased since electronic tests for honesty have become illegal in most situations.

In psychological testing, experts have determined that test scores predict job performance. In the jargon of testing professionals, your test behavior has a "correlation" with your working behavior—the two are interrelated. If one changes, so does the other. If your test results are significantly different from those of another candidate, your job performance will be, too—picking the person who tests "best" enables the employer to pick the most promising worker. That is the theory anyway, and in many cases a good test, properly administered and interpreted, can contribute something positive to an overall hiring decision.

Psychological testing is based on faith in the fact that the correlation between the test and the work to be done has been reasonably well established—studies of large groups of people who have taken the test, then attempted to do the job, bear out the expected results. That is to say, the test's developers have proven the "validity" of the test—it measures what they say it does. And they have proven the "reliability" of the test—it does so consistently, and not just for certain people.

The truth is that even the best psychological tests are limited in what they can predict. However, certain kinds of testing, in the hands of people who know and respect their limitations, can be useful. The problem is with the widespread use of psychological tests that are poorly constructed; oversold as simple, authoritative answers to complex questions; and abused by people who do not understand their limitations.

APTITUDE TESTS

While aptitude tests have often been rated among the best testing predictors of job success, there is criticism of them. Aptitude tests have cultural bias—they measure you in terms of your experiences in life, and people have unequal exposure to job-winning experiences. Another criticism is that the tests tell the obvious—people who have done well in other life experiences are the ones who will do well in future ones, such as new jobs. If past behavior is the best predictor of future behavior, and it seems to be, why is it necessary to have elaborate testing procedures to select good workers?

The most widely used state employment test is the U.S. Labor Department's General Aptitude Test Battery, or GATB. It is a twelve-part examination to predict workers' performance with a series of manual and ability-to-think tests. It supposedly removes about 9 percent of the guesswork in hiring. The GATB is at the center of a controversy regarding whether it should be adjusted to offset the discriminatory impact it has on groups who score poorly. This is an example of how employment testing is a reflection of broader social issues that impact on what you will experience in the hiring process.

A representative general employment test that is heavily used in hiring is the ten-part Employee Aptitude Survey (EAS), which can be used in combinations to cover the relevant parts of your abilities in the following areas:

- verbal comprehension (use words meaningfully);
- numerical ability (work easily with numbers and perform simple arithmetic);
- visual pursuit (speed and accuracy in visually tracing lines through an entangled network);
- visual speed and accuracy (see small details quickly and accurately);
- space visualization (visualize forms in space and manipulate objects mentally);
- numerical reasoning (analyze logical relationships);
- verbal reasoning (analyze verbally stated facts);
- word fluency (flexibility and ease in verbal communication);
- manual speed and accuracy (make fine finger movements rapidly and accurately); and
- symbolic reasoning (manipulate abstract symbols mentally).

The test's technical manual tells employers what you should score to be successful in nearly sixty kinds of jobs, ranging from clerical to executive. You would be tested in a combination of ten areas that best predict success in the position for which you are applying.

HONESTY TESTING

You might be one of the millions of applicants to encounter a written honesty test. The questions are usually pretty straightforward, and the results are determined by patterns shown by your answers, not on your answers to individual questions. Reliability claims by some test publishers purport 88 percent accuracy, but it is recommended that employers use the tests only in conjunction with other measures, including thorough interviews and investigations. State and federal authorities are looking into the validity of written tests in much the same way they did with the electronic testing that was banned in 1989.

PERSONALITY TESTING

Personality tests are used to screen applicants on the basis of traits that sound troubling in a prospective employee—inability to relate to others, for example. On the other hand, the same tests are used to select a desirable personality type, such as an extrovert for a marketing position. While critics claim that some of the tests are flawed and poor predictors of job performance, employers widely use them, and you should be prepared for them. Here are some examples of questions you might encounter:

- How often do you tell the truth?
- How often do you make your bed?
- Do you think you are too honest to take something that is not yours?
- True or false: I like to create excitement.
- How much do you dislike doing what someone tells you to do?
- Do you feel guilty when you do something you should not do?
- True or false: A lot of times I went against my parents' wishes.
- Do you believe that taking paper or pens without permission from a place where you work is stealing?
- What percentage of the people you know are so honest they wouldn't steal at all?
- How often do you blush?
- Do you know people who have cheated on their income-tax returns?
- How easy is it to get away with stealing?
- On the average, how often during the week do you go to parties?

The tests can be helpful in limited situations when they are professionally ad-ministered and scored; their limitations are respected; and they are used along with other measures, such as thorough interviews and background checks. You should take a psychological test without undue concern for your performance. Keep in mind that the tests are only good at separating the extremes—the high and the low scorers. It is doubtful that you will fall into the bottom category and be rejected. If you end up at the top, you don't care whether the test is accurate or not—it strength-ens your case for being hired. In the most likely scenario, you score in the middle, neither high nor low, and you "pass" the test because the results were not conclusive enough to make you stand out. You end up ranking "normal," and that is good enough for most hiring situations.

PSYCHOLOGICAL INTERVIEW

You may have a private session with a psychologist. It could be a general screening interview or an opportunity to discuss the results of tests you have taken. In either case, treat it as one more job interview and apply the same rules and common sense that have already been recommended. Understand that psychology is an imprecise science that sorts out the extremes in human behavior. Your best strategy is to be "normal" in your behavior and answers. Avoid extreme positions and reflect your regular professional behavior and values. Do not feel as though you have to elabo-rate or bare your soul on every question.

Focus your responses on how the question fits your working situation. Under-stand that you have two modes of behaving—a work model where you are more dis-ciplined and formal, and a personal one where you are less restrained. While some personal revelations may be called for, you are applying for a job, and the psycho-logical evaluation should be based on how you would behave at work, not in the re-laxed and private world of your own time. Don't even think about "telling all" about your deepest personal self—that should not be the emphasis of an employment psy-chological interview. Keep your thinking and standards of behavior oriented toward the professional setting and you will avoid the pitfalls of most psychological proce-dures.

ROLE-PLAYING

For certain kinds of jobs you can expect to be "tested" by going through an exercise designed to reveal your behavior in a simulated work situation. The emphasis can vary from a manual-skills task to problem-solving, priority-setting, or dealing with other people. If you are confronted with such a "test," your best strategy is to relax and be yourself. Reflect the commonsense work qualities that would go with the position for which you are an applicant—leadership, team player, whatever the situation calls for. Keep in mind that the role-playing task is just a device for having you display your broader workplace abilities and character, not that particular skill.

INFORMAL "TESTS"

Your test can still be going on when you have nominally "finished" the interview and are touring the plant. Ron Gregg, CEO of an outdoor equipment company in Seattle, ended up selecting his production manager on that basis. He needed someone with a passionate devotion to detail. After interviews Gregg takes candidates on a company tour and pays close attention to their remarks and observations as they go along. He is quoted in "Check It Out," an article in *INC.*, as saying:

> If someone is vague in a description of his or her past job, it's a tip-off....We had to interview about a hundred people before we found our current production manager, who was the only candidate to remark on the stitching, fabrics used, and other details in our products.

The point of this example is that you can never let your guard down during the job interview process. Whether you are having lunch with your interviewer or looking at the workplace facilities, you are onstage and should be trying your best to evaluate what makes you look best. Good questions and keen observation during the interview would have given the applicant in the example just cited cues to what he or she should "appreciate" and the kinds of values he or she should reflect after the interview turned informal.

Handwriting Analysis

With the banning of electronic honesty testing, businesses have turned to handwriting analysis as a way to test honesty and gain character insight. Three thousand firms use graphology in trying to make informed hiring decisions. Handwriting analysts consider some three hundred factors, ranging from the size and stroke to the pressure of the pen and the slant of the letters. Small, cramped handwriting with a large signature is said to show someone who thinks little of himself or herself but tries to cover up by projecting a big image. Upright, evenly spaced letters suggest an analytical and controlled writer.

Handwriting analysis is being looked at with the same kind of skeptical scrutiny that lie detectors were a few years ago. If the tests continue to be widely used and people are denied employment on the basis of their results, regulation will surely follow.

Physiological Testing

You should not be surprised to be expected to submit to a drug test as part of your employment selection process. More than half the Fortune 500 companies use some form of drug testing as a condition of employment—not after you have been hired and show signs of drug addiction. "False positives" are a potential problem in any kind of physiological test—they can show that you have the condition when you do not. The issues of drug and AIDS/HIV testing are discussed in Chapter 8, "Interviewing and the Law."

The only realistic answer to interview questions such as "Will you submit to a drug or HIV test?" is to say yes. There is a practical matter to keep in mind. Inquiring about your willingness to test is not the same as scheduling you for a blood or urine specimen and the analysis that follows. You would be foolish to refuse testing up front as a matter of principle when there is a chance you will never undergo the test. It is only when testing is actually scheduled that you have to decide.

Tips for Taking Physiological Tests

- Get whatever information the company provides on drugs and foodstuffs that might alter the test unfavorably.

- Scrupulously list all substances that you have been taking that could affect the test.

- See if you have the option of having the screening done at a private professional clinic or through your personal physician, where your privacy is assured.

- Take whatever precautions you can, such as flushing your system with lots of water; test late in the day to avoid an overly concentrated specimen; and nail down every assurance possible that you will be treated professionally should you test as false positive.

Unfair Testing

As a practical matter, you can't do much as an individual to remedy the unfair effects of testing in the hiring process. Unless the testing practice involves something like the polygraph in a clearly prohibited application, you can hardly refuse to do it. The solutions have to come from the legislative and regulatory authorities who become troubled enough about abusive practices to control them. Your role is to make your elected officials aware if you experience discrimination on the basis of unfair testing.

If you conclude that an unreasonable testing requirement has kept you from getting a job with a company, you may want to consider letting the executive managers of that firm know. Anything from an unwarranted psychological grilling to the expectation of a drug or HIV test without proper assurances of confidentiality and means for addressing false positives can affect your hiring. If it does, make sure the top-level managers know what is happening at the screening level and why you feel it is damaging their chances of hiring people like you; they just might not be aware of the abusive practices and might do something about them.

SUMMARY CHECKLIST: TECHNOLOGY AND THE INTERVIEW

- Expect to encounter some science and some pseudoscience in the job interview process.

- Computer-based background checks are common.

- Expect to have your credit checked, probably your education and professional experience claims, and possibly your arrest record and other personal matters.

- Computer-assisted interviewing is a possibility, but not likely, although you should be prepared to show that you can use a personal computer.

- Satellite-linked interviewing is being used by some companies and universities—mostly high-tech at this point.

- Videotaped interviews are sometimes worthwhile, but be sure your prospective employer is interested in looking at one before you make the investment.

- Lie detector testing has been outlawed for applicants for most kinds of jobs.

- Psychological and aptitude tests have many limitations, but you may have to take one, and you will do better by responding from a business rather than a personal behavior frame of reference.

- Handwriting analysis has grown in popularity since electronic honesty testing has been banned in most cases.

- Physiological testing for drugs and AIDS/HIV is commonplace, and you have to take precautions to keep from having your character damaged by false positives.

7 USING THE INTERNET

Going on a job interview today without a reasonable awareness of the Internet is like showing up for work not wearing a significant article of clothing. You simply aren't complete without it, and it could prove to be embarrassing.

How much you need to know varies, of course, with the job you seek and the market in which you are competing. Provincial jobs and companies still exist, but they grow fewer by the day. Web commerce, information, and communications make the Internet relevant to almost everyone, everywhere.

If the Internet is relevant to companies who hire, it is relevant to the people who want to work for them. As a job seeker the Internet can help you:

- Learn more about resume and letter writing
- Get career advice
- Find employers interested in hiring you
- Present your resume to the world (or selected parts of it) at little or no cost
- Communicate instantly by e-mail with employers and others who can help
- Research career opportunities, salaries, and working conditions
- Train for a new job or specialty
- Stay current in your field
- Learn more about the company to which you are applying
- Examine the cost of living and view homes where you consider moving

- Map your way to an interview and make travel arrangements
- Have an initial interview

At a minimum, if you don't have personal access to the Internet, find an acquaintance who does or go to a library where it is available and familiarize yourself with it. In a short time you can remove the mystery that separates you from those who have experienced the Web. It isn't necessary to spend much time or become an Internet enthusiast to grasp how it works and get a feel for its key features.

Looking over someone's shoulder, you can take a tour that leaves you comfortably aware of what a "search engine" is and what it can do, and that's half the battle. Enter a few topics and appreciate the sheer volume of information presented. Click some hyperlinks and see how one thing leads to another on the Internet. Armed with that brief experience you become a different person, better prepared to take your place in the new world of high-tech job hunting and employment.

If the only use you make of even superficial Internet exposure is in an interview saying, yes, you know what it is, your time was well spent. But there is so much more you can do to facilitate your job search.

This chapter is filled with illustrations, but a word of caution before you begin. Internet references are perishable; Internet addresses (URLs or Universal Resource Locations) change. Like telephone numbers and address changes in the non-cyber world, forwarding addresses (links, in the case of the Internet) are posted only for awhile. However, when they expire you can go to a search engine and enter keywords until you find the new address. If that fails, visit a site that logically might list the site you are looking for among its "suggested links." Web page sponsors pride themselves in referring visitors to their own favorites; the one you want or something better may be among those suggested.

Internet Tip

The table that follows lists a variety of URLs to check for help in your career search, resume writing, interviewing, salary negotiation, relocation, and other aspects of getting a job.

Illustrative Web Sites

What follows is a loose collection of useful information intended as starting points for what will quickly become your own original search. View these suggestions as a few places where you might first put your nose under the tent of Internet job search. Any one of them will start you on a journey that can easily last for hours, criss-crossing and interlacing the topics listed, and unearthing others that may be even more relevant to your particular needs and interests. Should you find a URL expired or need a different emphasis, go to a search engine and begin entering keywords: "maps," "real estate," "travel reservations," "white pages," "yellow pages," "zip codes," or whatever you need—it is probably there for the asking.

If your appetite for job search information is not satisfied after exploring these links, try http://www.dogear.com where for a modest fee you can purchase several thousand bookmarks to job-hunting sites that can be downloaded and clicked without typing URLs. The list is updated regularly and you are alerted by e-mail when revisions are available.

USEFUL JOB SEARCH INTERNET SITES		
Topic Keywords	**URL**	**Comments**
area codes	http://decoder. americom.com/	Returning a call to an unfamiliar area code? Identify the city by entering the area code at this site.
business newspapers	http://www.amcity.com	Examine specialty business papers serving 40 leading cities for general information and networking contacts.
career advice	http://www.washington post.com/parachute	*What Color Is Your Parachute* author Richard Nelson Bolles's Web page is filled with recommended links.
	http://jobsmart.org/	Resumes and more, including salary surveys.

(cont'd)

Topic Keywords	URL	Comments
career advice *cont'd*	http://stats.bls.gov/ ocohome.htm	The Department of Labor's *Occupational Outlook Handbook* online describes nearly every job you can imagine and discusses pay, working conditions, the demand for workers, expected education, where to go for more information, etc.
	http://www.careerweb. com	Job search, career-management advice, and more.
	http://www.dbm.com/	Click "Site Map" and go to articles and a great guide to Web job hunting.
careers	http://www.usnews.com/ usnews/edu/beyond/ bccguide.htm	*U. S. News & World Report's* excellent collection of career articles, advice, hot jobs, and salary information for entry-level candidates.
	http://careers.wsj.com/	Salaries, advice, articles, and more. Also features *Korn/Ferry Futurestep,* an appraisal of your market value by a preeminent search firm.
college job placement	http://www.jobtrak.com	A site serving prospective college grads and alumni at more than 700 colleges. Professional advice.

(cont'd)

Topic Keywords	URL	Comments
company information	http://www.hoovers.com/	Research a company: Free capsule, financials, and news or you can enter the keyword "investing" in a search engine and find sites with links to other company research resources.
company search	http://pic2.infospace.com/ _1_244791928_/_info. jbank/bizweb.htm	Find any company's Web page using this site.
dictionary and the-saurus	http://www.mw.com/ netdict.htm	Look it up in this giant on-line reference.
employment	http://www.nbew.com/	*National Business Employment Weekly*'s Web page includes the expected job search features plus an index of Web job listings.
equal opportunity	http://www.eeoc.gov/	Everything you need to know about EEO rights.
foreign language trans-lator	http://babelfish.altavista. digital.com/cgi-bin/ translate	Enter a phrase and get a translation.
health care info	http://www.dol.gov/dol/ pwba/public/health.htm	Department of Labor's consumer information on health care rights.
interviewing	http://iamag.com/ infoage/virtual.htm	"CU-SeeMe" interviewing mainly for technology-related positions.

(cont'd)

Topic Keywords	URL	Comments
interviewing *cont'd*	http://www.golden.net/~archeus/intres.htm#articles2	Links to interview sites that are reviewed for value and relevance.
	http://www1.kaplan.com/view/article/0,1275,536,00.html	Advice on preparing for your interview.
IRS forms and instructions	http://www.irs.ustreas.gov/prod/forms_pubs/index.html	Download tax forms and instructions.
job listings	http://www.ajb.dni.us/	Department of Labor Public Employment Service job/resume posting site. National and regional job search capabilities—the Web's version of the local employment office.
	http://headhunter.net/	An advertising-supported Web job and resume posting site.
	http://www.wm.edu/csrv/career/stualum/jregion.html	Links to listings by region of the country.
	http://www.washingtonpost.com/jobs	An example of a big city newspaper listing with extensive job search resources of its own.
	http://www.jobbankusa.com/	Links to everywhere in the job search universe.

(cont'd)

Topic Keywords	URL	Comments
job market	http://stats.bls.gov/blshome.html	The Bureau of Labor Statistics's latest numbers relating to status and trends in all sectors of the labor market.
	http://www.dol.gov/	Department of Labor laws, regulations, statistics, data, and news.
job search	http://www.jobweb.org/catapult/catapult.htm	National Association of Colleges and Employers links to useful job information.
	http://www.career.vt.edu/INTERNET/WEBHEAD.html	Virginia Tech's links to regions and occupational specialties. Other colleges have similar services—try your alma mater.
	http://www.job-hunt.org/	An extensive index of job search web sites complete with evaluations of usefulness.
letters	http://www.careerlab.com/	General advice and over 200 model letters on nearly every topic.
maps	http://www.mapquest.com/	Maps and directions to your interview.
pension information	http://www.dol.gov/dol/pwba/public/pension.htm	Department of Labor's consumer information on pension rights.

(cont'd)

Topic Keywords	URL	Comments
pension guarantees	http://www.pbgc.gov/	Pension Benefit Guarantee Corporation information on pension rights.
polygraph	http://www.dol.gov/dol/asp/public/programs/handbook/eppa.htm	Employee Polygraph Protection Act—your related rights.
resume advice	http://provenresumes.com/	Tips for various kinds of resumes including types of occupations and electronic formats.
	http://www.eresumes.com/	Electronic resumes are this page's specialty.
retirement benefits	http://www.dol.gov/dol/asp/public/programs/handbook/erisa.htm	ERISA and related laws to protect your pension.
salary information	http://www.dbm.com/jobguide/salary.html	Salary surveys, negotiation strategies, and more.
	http://jobsmart.org/tools/salary/salprof.htm/	Salary surveys by professional category.
search engines	http://www.metacrawler.com	Six search engines in one. Also try *Yahoo! HotBot, Infoseek, Exite, Lycos, Magellan,* etc., and examine their individual career sections that link you to many other sites.
	http://www.albany.net/allinone/all1www.html	A constantly updated index of specialized search engines—more than 100.

(cont'd)

Topic Keywords	URL	Comments
time zones	http://www.mich.com/ ~timezone/	Find the current time in a distant city before you call.
travel information	http://www.biztravel.com	Check flights, make reservations of all kinds, and optimize travel incentive programs.

Limitations

While the Internet is a wonderful source of career information, it has limitations. Use it with the same cautions you would apply outside cyberspace:

- If confidentiality is important to you, investigate and understand the safeguards job posting services employ before giving them your resume.

- Be sensible in offering personal information on the Internet. Employment listings are generally legitimate, but be skeptical enough to protect your privacy and personal safety. Verify with whom you are dealing before providing personal information or meeting a stranger for an interview. Don't become paranoid, but use common sense.

- Expect to be spammed (receive unsolicited commercial e-mail) if your e-mail address appears on the Internet. It is, unfortunately, the price you pay for using the Web.

- Understand that Internet job search works best for hard-to-find technical people. To judge how many responses your Internet resume is apt to attract, ask yourself how many calls you already receive from headhunters. Unless your telephone regularly rings and an executive recruiter is on the other end of the line, posting your credentials on the Internet may be disappointing. Employers seldom pay recruiters or search the Web for vacancies they can fill from ordinary print advertising that is cheaper and documents fair hiring practices compliance.

- Anyone can represent him or herself as a career expert on the Internet. Evaluate them as you would any other service before following advice that may lead you where you don't want to go or before buying ineffective goods and services.

With those few words of caution, by all means explore and make the most of the job search riches of the Internet. Remember, there is more than resume posting that might prove helpful in your job search.

SUMMARY CHECKLIST: USING THE INTERNET

- At the very least, give yourself a cursory tour of the Internet to familiarize yourself with how and what its key features are.

- Because URLs are perishable, use search engines to locate Web sites for topics whose addresses have changed or expired or when you do not have a direct address.

- Use the Internet to research companies on both general sites and on individual companies' Web sites.

- Keep in mind that resumes posted on the Internet are most successful for highly qualified people seeking specialized technical positions.

- Understand the confidentiality limitations of posting your resume on the Internet.

- Be cautious about offering personal information and purchasing services without checking the background of a company or an individual.

- In addition to career-specific topics, don't overlook the general reference potential of the Internet in supporting your job search and interviews.

8 | INTERVIEWING AND THE LAW

You have rights in the job market, but exercising them can be a delicate proposition; good judgment is required. In this chapter you are made aware of broad legal and regulatory concepts that protect you from unreasonable discrimination. You will see that there is legitimate concern behind many "improper" questions, and you should deal with them positively instead of announcing your right to sue. You will be better able to judge your interviewer's intentions and respond effectively without compromising either your rights or your chances of getting the job. And just in case you do encounter the real thing—blatant, damaging employee selection discrimination—you are told where to go for specific help in fighting back.

While discrimination is the dominant issue, it is not the only area where legal matters can have an impact your job interviewing success. Topics covered in this chapter include:

- equal employment opportunity;
- credit checks;
- privacy; and
- job references.

As you will see, these issues have a tendency to intermingle and overlap. You should be aware of what is right and what is wrong in the employee selection process, but view them in a practical job hunter's context—not an attorney's. Your objective throughout your search is to get the job you want. The law is there if you really need it, and most interviewers act in good faith. But that does not mean you should endure sexual harassment or any other threatening behavior by an interviewer. You are just encouraged to be practical and go with the flow when the intent is not mean-spirited and you can help your cause with a more expansive answer than you might technically have to give.

Equal Employment Opportunity

Employers are not allowed to discriminate against you on the basis of race, color, sex, religion, national origin, or age. The federal agency that administers this policy is the Equal Employment Opportunity Commission (EEOC). It enforces:

- Title VII of the Civil Rights Act of 1964;
- the Age Discrimination in Employment Act of 1967;
- the Equal Pay Act of 1963; and
- Section 501 of the Rehabilitation Act of 1973.

As the names imply, Title VII insures your civil rights, the next prevents age discrimination (if you are over forty), the third outlaws unequal pay for men and women doing the same work, and Section 501 represents your interests if you are handicapped. You can obtain detailed information on any of these statutes by contacting your local EEOC agency or by dialing 1-800-USA-EEOC. For purposes of this book, it is enough for you to know the basics—these kinds of discrimination are illegal, and you have advocates and remedies. The last section of this chapter tells you how to get help.

Internet Tip

The Internet source for Equal Employment Opportunity information is http://www.eeoc.gov/.

SEXUAL HARASSMENT

You should be aware that it is illegal under federal laws administered by the EEOC to harass people sexually in the workplace. If your fundamental rights to seek employment are interfered with by sexual coercion, you may have the basis for a complaint.

The EEOC issued guidelines in 1980 that make sexual harassment in the workplace illegal. In 1986 the U.S. Supreme Court unanimously affirmed those rights and spelled out the two types of sexual harassment that can be the subject of legal redress:

- *Quid pro quo* is the most blatant form of "environmental" sexual abuse, and it can be verbal and not just physical in form. In this situation you are expected to trade sex for the privilege of obtaining, keeping, or getting promoted in your job.

- *Hostile working environment* is the other, more subjective half of the sexual harassment equation. Here you are placed in a work environment that makes it difficult to do your job. The actions of your coworkers create a hostile or offensive environment and, in effect, deny you the right to go about your business of doing a good job without undue emphasis on your sex.

Writing in *Time* soon after the Clarence Thomas–Anita Hill Senate hearings, Nancy Gibbs tried to put the issue in perspective:

> ...sexual harassment is not about civility. It is not about a man making an unwelcome pass, telling a dirty joke or commenting on someone's appearance. Rather it is an abuse of power in which a worker who depends for her livelihood and professional survival on the goodwill of a superior is made to feel vulnerable. "This is not automatically a male-female issue," says Wendy Reid Crisp, the director of the National Association for Females Executives...."We define this issue as economic intimidation."

The reality is that most problems with sexual harassment occur between a female subordinate and a male supervisor. You cannot be overly sensitive to the routine sparks that will always fly between the sexes—even when it happens at work and even when it takes a tasteless form. The Ninth U.S. Circuit Court in California ruled that judgment is required. Behavior subject to redress under the law would have to be that which would offend a "reasonable woman."

An accompanying *Time* poll showed that 34 percent of women answered yes to the question, "Have you ever experienced what you regard as sexual harassment at work?" Still, only 5,557 complaints were filed with the EEOC on the issue that year. It is clearly a difficult issue with all manner of practical considerations for women and men at work. As many articles on the subject conclude, it is much like the issue of pornography—people can't define it, but they know it when they see it. If you see it in your job interview, be aware that it is an increasingly unacceptable practice in our society and, if it denies you the right to employment, you have rights that should be pursued.

With that said, you are left with the day-to-day reality of sex in the workplace. Much of the dynamism in our modern workforce is sexual energy that is not meant to be coercive or even offensive. Understanding each other takes effort, good communication, and optimism about the pleasures of working together once we find our way around the obvious obstacles. Read Chapter 9, "Sex and the Interview," for a less litigious discussion of the issue. Should your interests in workplace relationships go deeper, you are advised to read a book that I coauthored on the subject, titled *More Than Friends, Less Than Lovers: Managing Sexual Attraction in the Workplace* (Jeremy P. Tarcher, 1991).

DEALING WITH ILLEGAL INQUIRIES

You are only allowed to be asked information that is directly related to your ability to perform the job for which you are applying. Here are some things you probably should not be asked about:

- racial or ethnic background;
- religious affiliation, church attended, religious holidays observed;
- national origin, where parents, spouse, or relatives are from—native language;
- marital status; or
- number of children.

Employers may try to get at this information indirectly by asking about:

- a woman's maiden name;
- place of birth;
- social clubs;
- hobbies;
- person to notify in case of emergency; and
- photographs.

Keep in mind that many states have their own lists of questions that can and cannot be asked in preemployment interviews. You should inquire locally if you have a concern about improper questioning in your jurisdiction. Following are guidelines for dealing with sensitive employer questions. The suggested answers show your willingness to address an employer's honest concerns but not to be discriminated against.

HEALTH

Instead of asking you what health-related problems you have, the interviewer can inquire whether you have any condition that would prevent you from doing the job. Rather than refusing to answer the question, your answer can be a straightforward assurance that you have no health conditions that would limit your ability to do the job.

CRIMINAL RECORD

In the case of criminal records, the employer can ask if you have any pending indictments, since that could be relevant to your availability for work. The nature of the crime might make a difference in determining your desirability for the position and is a legitimate question, too. In most states you can be asked if you have been convicted of a crime, but that alone cannot keep you from being hired. Your employer would have to consider the nature and seriousness of the crime, when the crime occurred, and show that it has relevance to the job.

RELIGION

Your interviewers' concern with religion is probably a practical one. They want to know whether your faith would keep you from being available for work at important times. While they are prevented from asking about your religion, they are within their rights to inquire about your availability to work on certain days. You can help an interview if such a line of questioning drifts off the mark by responding that your beliefs are a very private matter for you, but you can assure them that they would not interfere with your work schedule or ability to perform your duties.

NATIONAL ORIGIN

You cannot be asked about your ancestry or the status of your family in the immigration and naturalization process, but it is proper to establish whether you are a citizen of the United States. Employers are required to do so. If a job requires knowledge of a foreign language, a direct inquiry about your language skills is proper. If language skill is not a requirement and the inquiry is used to uncover national origin, your interviewer has probably broken the law.

AGE

Your interviewer can establish that you are age eighteen or older, and that is about all. If you encounter the "How old are you?" question, answer it by making your age a strength—couch your response in terms of experience and ability to do the job better.

MARITAL AND FAMILY SITUATION

"Are you married?" and "Do you plan to have children?" questions are illegal, but they often show more ignorance of the law than bad faith. Try assuming that it shows an honest concern about you quitting soon to raise a family. Consider giving the response that the interviewer is looking for without feeling obligated to elaborate. Volunteer that you separate work and family obligations and see no problem meeting the expected work hours or travel obligations. In those rare instances where such a line of questioning persists, politely ask that relevancy be established if you are expected to provide details about your personal life. Only a naïve interviewer would push the issue further, and if you have been careful, no harm was done to your hiring prospects.

Tips for Answering Questions

Your best approach to fending off an improper question is the polite three-step procedure that:

- answers any question that won't do you harm;
- makes an inoffensive aside that you had the impression such questions were illegal; and
- avoids threatening the interviewer or labeling yourself litigious.

Correctly done, this procedure clears the air on potentially sensitive issues that could be damaging if left unanswered, lets it be known that you are aware of your rights (and discourages further improper questioning), and keeps the goodwill of your interviewers by giving them an easy way out of something that could have gotten them into trouble.

Credit Checks

The Fair Credit Reporting Act protects you from certain kinds of credit investigations that might be associated with your application for a job. In general, routine credit checks are acceptable, but "investigative consumer reports" that involve interviewing people who know you are not, unless you are notified. Laws vary by state, so check your local situation if you suspect discrimination. When you sign most job applications, you authorize a credit check. It will mention investigative consumer reports if the inquiry is to go beyond the routine report.

Privacy

Your rights to privacy are protected by the Fourth Amendment to the Constitution, and it is the basis for limiting unreasonable preemployment inquiries. A discussion of some of the key privacy issues as they relate to your situation as a job candidate follows. A few of them have regulatory remedies; others are just becoming visible enough sources of abuse to warrant scrutiny. The objective is not to alarm you, but to prepare you for the possibility that you will be confronted with these procedures. Knowing that the issues exist will alert you to possible harm and steer you toward a rational approach to dealing with the challenge.

DRUG TESTING

Following abuse by employers, the courts and states are establishing limits that focus testing on certain professions where public safety is at risk and where there are grounds to suspect drug use. The EEOC does not have specific policies on drug testing, but it will investigate on a case-by-case basis charges alleging that testing procedures adversely and unjustly impact on the hiring of minorities or women.

AIDS/HIV

Job candidates with AIDS/HIV may have certain rights under laws that protect the handicapped, and you should check with the EEOC for details in this rapidly evolving field.

HONESTY TESTS

The Employee Polygraph Protection Act of 1988 ended routine use of the polygraph except in a limited number of occupations and where there is some basis for suspecting wrongdoing. "Voice stress analyzers" are included in the prohibitions of the polygraph act. Here are the highlights of what you should know about the Employee Polygraph Protection Act:

- It prohibits most private employers from using lie detector tests for pre-employment screening.

- Employers are generally prohibited from requiring or requesting any job applicant to take a lie detector test.

- While local laws and collective bargaining agreements can be more restrictive, federal law says that federal, state, and local governments are not affected by the law. It does not apply to tests given by the federal government to private individuals engaged in national security-related activities.

- Polygraph tests can be administered in the private sector to prospective employees of security service firms (armored car, alarm, and guard) and of pharmaceutical manufacturers, distributors, and dispensers.

- Polygraph testing is also allowed when there is reasonable suspicion of private workplace theft, embezzlement, etc.

- If you are examined, you have rights relating to the length of the test, written notice before testing, the right to refuse or discontinue a test, and the right not to have the results disclosed to unauthorized persons.

- For additional information or to file a complaint, look in your local telephone directory under U.S. Government, Department of Labor, Employment Standards Administration, Wage and Hour Division.

Pencil and paper tests are not prohibited, and that includes "graphology" or handwriting analysis. They are still legal, and the EEOC will entertain only case-by-case complaints on tests used in a discriminatory manner.

Internet Tip

The Internet source for polygraph rights information is
http://www.dol.gov/dol/asp/public/programs/handbook/eppa.htm

GENETIC SCREENING

While the practice is not widespread, you can add to your list of concerns the use of new tests to discriminate against job candidates whose genetic traits make them susceptible to certain diseases.

Job References

If you experience difficulty in getting job references, it may be because they have become the source of so much litigation. According to a *U.S. News & World Report* article by Jo Ann Tooley:

> Employers are so wary of lawsuits from disgruntled ex-employees that over half of the firms surveyed said they would not give out any information at all on former employees without their written consent. In fact, 10 percent are so cautious that they never provide references. And with good cause: Defending a defamation suit before a jury can cost as much as $250,000, even if the company prevails....Nearly a third of all libel cases come from workers who sue former employers over bad references. A recent survey of 694 employers shows that bosses are becoming tight-lipped as a result.

As a job candidate you should keep in mind that a former employer can say anything that is justified by your personnel files. Poor performance is a legitimate cause for dismissal, and information relating to you can be shared in an objective way. If the facts and records back it up "you can feel free to challenge an ex-employee's ability or integrity and even imply criminality...." According to specialists in defending employers against defamation suits, your ex-employer can say anything about you if his facts and records back it up. You are never well advised to go looking for unwarranted litigation. What you want to remember about job reference wrongdoing is that you have redress if you find yourself among the few whose careers are unfairly damaged by a malicious reference.

Where to Go for Help

If you feel that you have encountered serious discrimination and want to do something about it, you need to be aware that there are time limits on filing. The best advice is to act promptly. Identify the local agency that deals with enforcing antidiscrimination laws and call it for guidance. When that is not possible, your next option is to call the federal 1-800-USA-EEOC help number and ask what to do next. To give you some appreciation of the process, here is how the EEOC handles a complaint:

1. The EEOC interviews the potential charging party to obtain as much relevant information as possible about the alleged discrimination. If all legal jurisdictional requirements are met, a charge is properly drafted, and the investigative procedure is explained to the charging party (you).

2. The EEOC then notifies the employer about the charge. In investigating the charge to determine if discrimination occurred, the EEOC requests specific information from the employer tailored to address the issues directly affecting the charging party as well as other potentially aggrieved persons. Any witnesses who have direct knowledge of the alleged discriminatory act will be interviewed. If evidence shows there is no reasonable cause to believe discrimination occurred, the charging party and the employer will be notified. The charging party may request a review of a no-cause finding by EEOC headquarters officials. The charging party also may exercise the right to bring private court action.

3. If the evidence shows there is reasonable cause to believe discrimination occurred, EEOC conciliates or attempts to persuade the employer to eliminate the discrimination voluntarily, following the standards of the EEOC's Policy on Remedies and Relief for Individual Cases of Unlawful Discrimination. Remedies may include reinstatement of the charging party to the job he or she would have had but for the discrimination, back pay, restoration of lost benefits, and a notice posted by the employer in the workplace to advise employees that it has complied with orders to remedy the discrimination.

4. The EEOC considers the case for litigation if conciliation fails. If approved by the commission, the EEOC will file a lawsuit in federal district court on behalf of the charging party or parties. The charging party or parties may intervene in the EEOC's suit. Charging parties may initiate private civil action on their own in lieu of EEOC litigation.

In a nutshell, you have a powerful advocate who will try to determine the merits of your case, get the problem solved out of court if possible, and sue on your behalf if a simpler solution cannot be found. You keep the right to take action privately. For it all to work, you have to meet the deadlines set up in the various statutes. So if you have a serious complaint, establish contact early and determine precisely what you must do and when.

Keep in mind that the laws relating to many of these issues are constantly evolving. For areas such as AIDS/HIV and drug testing, you are advised to check the information services of the national advocacy groups who monitor the situation for their constituents and who can advise you of the most current conditions.

SUMMARY CHECKLIST: INTERVIEWING AND THE LAW

- You have to balance using your legal rights with your objective of getting the job.

- Employees are not allowed to discriminate against you on the basis of race, color, sex, religion, national origin, or age.

- Preemployment questioning risks being illegal unless it relates to your ability to do the job.

- As a practical matter, you should answer any reasonable question that won't harm your chances of being hired.

- Routine credit checks are generally permitted, while "investigative consumer reports" require your consent.

- Most preemployment testing is legal unless it can be shown to discriminate against protected classes such as minorities, women, the handicapped, or people over forty.

- Lie detectors are illegal except for limited special applications.

- Job reference givers can be liable for suits based on defamation and wrongful discharge or termination.

- Look for advice on the violation of your preemployment rights at your local equal employment agency, or call 1-800-USA-EEOC.

- AIDS/HIV, drug abuse testing, and other special-interest concerns are best addressed by national help lines operated for their constituents.

9

SEX AND THE INTERVIEW

Sexual chemistry is something you might not be able to avoid encountering in your job interview; it happens. Attraction can be a pleasantly helpful addition to communication or a distasteful intrusion on the objectivity of your interview. It all depends on the quality of your experience, which might range from a polite compliment to a sleazy pass. While sex and the interview is nothing to be paranoid about, awareness is healthy, and you should be ready *if* attraction finds its way into your job interview. How you cope with it could affect the outcome of your interview—and even your career.

The author would like to acknowledge that, in spite of his best efforts at being sensitive and enlightened, what you are about to read in this particular chapter has a male bias that is apparently impossible to remove. With that said, and readers alerted to be selective in the advice they choose, it remains the opinion of the author that there is value in considering his points. If no other purpose is served, women may gain insight into how a man views their plight, and in so doing improve their skills for dealing with him in ways that they know better than he to be effective.

The composition of the work force has changed in recent years, but human biology has remained the same. Whether you are a woman or a man interviewing for a job today, you stand an excellent chance of finding yourself interacting with attractive members of the opposite sex—many of them authority figures able to influence your hiring. You need to manage the sexual chemistry that can arise quite naturally and not let it get in the way of communicating your fundamental professional suitability for the job. Actress Julia Roberts put it this way in a magazine interview:

Sexual tension is everywhere. I feel it and I support it. I don't partake of it all the time. If I had a meeting with ten men for a movie that I really wanted, the last thing I would think about is, do they find me attractive? I'm too busy trying to convince these people of the points I'm there trying to make. That's why I don't get that kind of stuff that you hear happens to actresses. You get what you give out, and maybe seven times out of ten, if that situation comes up, it's because somebody was giving off a funky energy that somebody else was picking up on and that person decided to seize the moment. I don't ever put that out there unless it's a normal situation of trying to woo some guy.

If you do decide to use sex to your advantage while interviewing, you will want to do so skillfully, tastefully, and with a realistic awareness of the downside risks as well.

Classic Situations

When sex finds its way into a job interview, it is usually through a familiar door. You can recognize it, analyze it, and decide how best to deal with it in light of your personal situation and values. There is no single correct way—each case is a judgment call. But there is a pattern that you can expect to be part of, and knowing your role can preempt surprise and have you prepared to react in your own best interests. Sexual communication is a delightful human phenomenon, and most men and women can enjoy it while still respecting the essential boundaries. But for those who cannot, you need to have your defenses ready.

INTERVIEWER-INITIATED SEXUAL ATTRACTION

When men and women confront each other privately—as in a job interview session—there is often sexual communication that dominates their dialogue for an instant until the social protocols take over and put their meeting on a more objective plane. You tend to appraise each other's attractiveness and, some would say, revert to the ancient anthropologically imprinted process of assessing each other's mating potential. It brings energy and charm to our interaction with one another—if it stops there or settles into a pattern acceptable to both parties. It is when you find yourself coerced or exploited by what should be a perfectly natural but fleeting experience that you have to be careful. Here is a way to evaluate your situation and deal with it appropriately.

OVERT CONFRONTATION

Sleazy male/female interaction is disturbing, but it can still happen. If someone propositions you in the course of a job interview, be surprised—he or she has probably just placed his or her job in jeopardy. At least in large organizations, you should find people sufficiently enlightened not to come on with an old-fashioned pass. In addition to being of questionable legality under equal opportunity regulations, such behavior is generally considered gauche. While it is always possible that two people will meet in this way, find each other utterly irresistible, and go on to share the love of a lifetime, in most cases it is calculated, objectionable, and almost certainly illegal if it affects your rights to be hired on the merits.

If you encounter up-front sexual aggressiveness at an interview, you have to decide whether you would want to work in an organization that tolerates such behavior. If you do, fine—that is still one way to get a job. Chances are you are not interested, in which case you can point out that you are there for a job and not a date and that his or her behavior is inappropriate. If that doesn't bring an apology followed by an objective interview, leave and think about whether you want to make an issue of the incident with the interviewer's superior or forget the whole thing. If the superior is indifferent, you have the option of pursuing the matter with senior management or the local office of the Equal Employment Opportunity Commission.

Overt sexual confrontation in a job interview bodes poorly for your chances of having a successful and satisfying career with that organization. Unless you get immediate and convincing satisfaction when you make your objections known, look elsewhere for work. It is up to you whether you want to try to fix the problem for others coming after you by making your experience known to those who might correct the situation. If you do, and you probably should, be very objective and careful about what you say. Describe the behavior you encountered, your reaction to it, and why you elected not to pursue employment after that; do not attack the individual personally or make the incident into more than it was. Truth is the absolute defense for libel or slander—the charges you might face if you damage the interviewer's career. Do not let the prospect of this discourage you; just be careful how you make your charges. If you can find other people who have shared your experience, so much the better. Ask the supervisor if there have been other complaints, and make note of his or her response in case you need it later.

SUBTLE ADVANCES

Any encounter you have with workplace discrimination at the front door of the hiring process is apt to be more subtle. Innuendo replaces the proposition, and you are left to deal with a veiled threat. What sounds like a compliment at first persists or recurs after you field the initial overture with a polite turnoff. In the worst case, your interviewer becomes your antagonist and escalates his or her interest into suggestions that he or she can help you or make your job search much easier if you accept his or her interest in you.

Once again, you are advised to make your decision regarding whether these are the terms of employment that you are willing to accept. Assuming that you would not, you are left in the uncomfortable position of trying to convince the interviewer that your interest is in employment and not a personal relationship. If that is possible, proceed with the interview. If the subtle advances continue, leave the session and decide whether it is worth protesting. Your first recourse is in-house. If that fails, the Equal Employment Opportunity Commission is there to hear your complaint.

Subtle discrimination is harder to confront than overt. Still you should seriously consider making your feelings known to management. You may be contributing to a cumulative case against a person who should not be in a position of authority, and you might get him or her removed. As much as you might need the job, there are almost certainly better alternatives than the kind of compromise that pandering to unwanted attraction entails.

INNOCENT ATTRACTION

The only kind of sexual attraction that can have its charm and deserve some tolerance on your part is the innocent kind—you will know it when you see it. There are times when your interviewer is simply smitten. He or she is a nice guy or gal but just cannot get over the fact that he is dealing with a beautiful woman (or she with a handsome man)—and it shows. This is when you might actually have an advantage and not want to destroy it with oversensitivity. You can tell the difference between someone who is trying to take advantage of the situation by leveraging a favorable job interview into a personal relationship and the person who just shows an awkward interest.

You are advised to play the innocent interviewer carefully, but with some benefit of the doubt. If it turns out to be a ploy and the hardball sexual manipulation begins, revert to the overt and subtle action defenses described above. It is just as likely, however, that you are in a totally manageable situation where you can let the personal charm work to your advantage. Be careful not to encourage anything—that almost certainly won't be necessary. Just be polite and charming and make your objective case with the added backdrop of letting the interviewer be impressed with you personally.

There are no rules that say job interviews have to be antiseptic and devoid of feelings or subtle communication—including innocent sexual attraction. Unless you find yourself in an offensive situation, relax and use the open channel to convey liking and warmth that are appropriate to the setting. Body language almost always has sexual overtones, and they don't have to be "bad."

Control is the secret to managing the sexual component of a job interview. As long as you feel you have it and are comfortable with the game you are sharing, there is no need to erect boundaries that protect all that the law will allow. The laws are there to defend you from abuse, not to prevent you from exerting influence in a healthy, natural, voluntary way. Any time a man and a woman interact, sex is in the air between them. Your job interview is no exception, and all it takes is good judgment and a careful reading of the situation to use it to your tasteful advantage. Every member of the opposite sex who finds you attractive in the course of doing business doesn't mean to offend or take inappropriate liberties with you—count to ten, protect your interests, listen to your instincts about the bad ones, but be ready to use your natural advantage when it surfaces in the right way.

Guidelines for Handling Interviewer-Initiated Sexual Attraction

- Begin with self-analysis and know your own position on how you will use your attractiveness before coming into the interview.

- Without overreacting, be sensitive to your potential for inviting what you may not want and avoid it—don't shy away from looking your best and wearing flattering clothes, but don't go to extremes.

- Start with your professional bearing dominant, easing into a more personal tone only after you are comfortable doing so—when you have established that the interviewer will not leap to the wrong conclusions.

- After a warmup period, if attraction seems to be playing a role in the session, assess your interviewer as overt, subtle, or innocent.

- In the case of overt and subtle interviewers:
  - ✓ begin by ignoring the overtures and not encouraging them with even remotely favorable responses;
  - ✓ if that fails, ask that the advances stop and an objective interview continue;
  - ✓ if unsuccessful, leave the interview and ask to see the interviewer's superior to make him or her aware of the problem; and
  - ✓ finally, if nothing else has been effective, decide whether it is worth seeking satisfaction at the senior management level or the EEOC.

- In the case of the innocent interviewer:

✓ make a character judgment and test it to see if he or she remains in character or deteriorates with modest encouragement;

✓ if you establish that you are dealing with a charmed but restrained member of the opposite sex, work with the person on enjoying the attraction while remaining sensitive to danger signals;

✓ subtly use the power of a discreetly shared attraction to open doors, develop needed insights into the position, amplify your objective qualifications for the job, and make yourself memorable; and

✓ avoid the temptation to lead, let the interviewer do that—your role is to respond with warmth and a degree of encouragement, not to take the initiative and trigger his or her defenses or suspicions of being manipulated.

CANDIDATE-INITIATED SEXUAL ATTRACTION

Sex works. There is just no doubt that it is influential in man/woman interactions, and that includes the business scene. You can use it to your advantage, just as countless numbers of your colleagues do every business day. But the task has grown more complex—the direct marketing of your attributes, as a man or woman, is more chancy that it might have been when the workplace population was less balanced. Today you have to be selective in the application of your sexual powers and careful not to offend—your target or those in the background who could take offense and damage your chances of success. You need to be sensitive and cultivate your skills in reading the situation correctly and applying your attributes judiciously. Here are a few suggestions.

OVERT BEHAVIOR

It would be a rare business situation these days where you would benefit by coming on as an overtly sexy candidate. Genuine attractiveness still sells, but not overtly, and it needs to be accompanied with real business skills if it is to lead anywhere except an affair.

Save the sexy clothes for later, and only at intervals. As an established member of the team, an occasional sexy look can set an interesting tone, if that's *not* all you've got. Unless you know with certainty that it will be well received and not forever limiting, don't dress sexy for your job interview. It is easy enough to show that you have the underlying potential without making a bold statement. If you are attractive, let it show, but modestly.

Guidelines for Handling Candidate-Initiated Sexual Attraction

- Decide what you have to offer and how it can most effectively be articulated in your job interview.

- Appraise the general interviewing audience, and balance your approach so that what impresses a few doesn't serve to turn off many.

- Use a subtle approach and present yourself as open to the complimentary interpretation of those you encounter—don't hit others over the head with your appeal, but don't totally deny its existence either.

- Recognize that sex appeal is in the eye of the beholder, and be prepared to communicate it innocently and let your attractiveness speak for itself.

Interview Sexuality and Common Sense

You really must have perspective if you are to deal effectively with sexual attraction in the workplace. All the laws and regulations in the world are not going to eliminate the inevitable chemistry between men and women—at work or anywhere else. You are left with the task of sorting it all out case by case.

- Is your interviewer being mean-spirited and planning to cause you continuing problems? Or is the person naïve and unaware of the impact he or she is having on you?

- Is the comment just a clumsy way to get at a valid business concern and, therefore, deserving of a creative answer that will get both of you off the hook? Or are you dealing with a sexist bigot?

- Do you have the gut feeling from the beginning that your professional talents will be dwarfed by the constant need to defend yourself against sexual innuendos and worse?

- Are you the one deliberately bringing the sexual emphasis to the interview, and have you exercised good judgment? Are you, therefore, setting yourself up for a fast return to the unemployment line?

PUTTING IT INTO PERSPECTIVE

Without compromising either your rights or your personal safety, you need to treat your interview as what it is: your opportunity to land a job. If sexual sensitivities get in the way of doing that, you are defeating your primary purpose. Here are some further points to assist you:

- If you as a man or a woman are asked about your spouse, consider the possibility that the interviewer has a valid business reason, and try to satisfy the concern. Your answer can focus on the professional and address whatever concerns you can imagine being important.

  ✓ Will your spouse be an asset in your business social obligations?

  ✓ Will you have an independent career free from the need to limit your growth to satisfy a spouse's ambitions?

- If asked about your plans to marry or raise a family, you can take the positive approach and respond that your plans are to pursue your career actively and on a full-time basis.

- If asked for a date or otherwise approached in an improperly personal way, give the interviewer a chance or two to reverse field, recognize that he or she is out of line, and salvage the interview for both of you.

SUMMARY CHECKLIST: SEX AND THE INTERVIEW

- Sexual energy can make a natural intrusion on your interview, and you need to be prepared to deal with it appropriately if it does.

- All manifestations of sexual attraction between an interviewer and applicant don't have to be negative and destructive ones.

- You have a degree of choice as to what role your sexual attractiveness will play in your job interview.

- Interviewer-initiated sexual attraction can be overt, subtle, or innocent, and each calls for a different response.

- There are steps you can take to diagnose correctly the nature of the sexualized interview you might experience.

- Perspective and common sense play major roles in judging the proper role of sexual attraction in your job interview.

- Seemingly improper questions can mask legitimate employer concerns, and you might voluntarily and selectively address them without yielding important rights.

10

SPECIAL SITUATIONS

If you find yourself out of step with the traditional career ladder—not clearly pursuing the next logical position in your field—this chapter can help you have a successful job interview. There are things you need to know about attitudes you might encounter and proven techniques to help you gain understanding and respect in your circumstances.

A special approach to the interview is needed for job seekers who enter the world of work from nontraditional situations. An employer advertising a vacancy usually expects to attract people who are working full time in a job closely aligned with the position being offered. For example, applicants for a senior management position are generally people already working as senior or middle managers in roughly the same kinds of settings as the job for which they are applying.

When you depart from the traditional career ladder, your approach to job interviewing has to compensate for your differences with what the employer expects. You try to anticipate the negative things and neutralize them by accentuating your strengths and minimizing your weaknesses. Prepare to do that well, and the very experiences that led you off the yellow brick road can actually make you more attractive than candidates with routine careers.

Among those who will find this chapter particularly useful are people who are:

- *returning to the workplace following an absence* caused by family obligations, a small business venture, involuntary loss of employment, or full-time study;

- *applying for a less prestigious job* than the one previously held due to organizational downsizing or a reduction in the work force;

- *students preparing for a first professional position,* including work-study
  arrangements, as a lead-in to a career position;

- *establishing a second career* following early retirement;

- *looking for flexibility* in hours or overall working arrangements; or

- *coming from another culture* and struggling to articulate the value of their
  work and training in alien settings.

Returning to the Workplace

Stepping out of the traditional career path is increasingly common. A free society
provides opportunities for uniquely personalized work lives, and many of us exercise those options. Another factor is that our rapidly evolving, competitive economy
does not necessarily guarantee job continuity throughout our lifetime.

Here are some reasons why you might find yourself sitting in a job interview explaining why you are coming to the job market with a less than traditional work history:

- a period of unemployment, self-employment, or part-time employment to
  raise a family;

- a small business or consulting venture of your own that is no longer as attractive as a traditional position;

- a merger or reorganization that leaves you unemployed; or

- a period of full-time study that was necessary to change careers or achieve
  the level of employment you wanted.

RECOMMENDED APPROACH

In each of these instances your approach to the job interview is one of being positive and objective. You do not attempt to hide your actual situation; neither do you
apologize for it. Determine what your marketable strengths are and decide how to
bring them to the attention of someone who can use them.

You are what you are—there is no need for, or anything to be gained by, postur-
ing as something else. If you are a homemaker who worked only briefly as a management trainee before spending ten years outside the workplace, then you are an

entry-level employee with some experience—*plus* a great deal of added maturity and motivation to bring to the next phase of your career.

There are ways for you to deal with the apparent negatives of your situation during a job interview. The following chart lists a few of the things you might face (openly or beneath the surface) and how you can compensate.

CHALLENGES AND RESPONSES FOR RETURNING WORKERS	
Challenge	**Response**
Your experience is out-of-date.	I have remained active in the marketplace as a consumer of your services and can bring that valued perspective to the job.
You are too old for this level position.	Think, act, and look young—this is usually more a problem of perception than reality. Chronological age has little to do with working age in most contemporary, nonphysically—demanding jobs.
Your education is dated.	Take a refresher course or seminar. It will not only bring you up-to-date on terminology, you also stand a good chance of networking with people who can help you find employment.

JOB INTERVIEWING TIPS

Market yourself very deliberately. Do your homework on the company and the job being offered. Put yourself in the hiring official's shoes and make a case for why you should be an attractive hire. You should be prepared to respond to the interviewer's questions and make points of your own during the interview that stress your competency and help to dismantle the myth of needing continuity through a series of lesser positions to do well in this one.

Couch your experience in terms and with examples that relate to the proposed work situation. If you are listing experience as a telephone volunteer for your alumni association fund drive or the local public television station, use terms such as "telemarketing"—translate your experience into the buzzwords of the business world so the interviewer doesn't have to. Portray yourself as someone:

- aware of what the position entails;
- qualified to perform the duties; and
- motivated to assume a realistic role in the company.

Before the hiring official begins recounting your precise experience and training, you want to make the point that you know what he or she wants and can provide it.

You need to have a selection of "competency clusters" or qualifications and achievements in mind that substantiate your claim. This is where your homework pays off—by knowing what the job actually entails, you have the advantage of being able to translate your strengths into those valued by the employer. You can describe an experience in general terms or in job-specific terms; the latter focuses employer attention on exactly what you can do for him or her, rather than relying on him or her to reach the same conclusion the hard way—by puzzling over your uninterpreted activities. Make the logical connection that your experience supports the company's needs—in that way you put the burden on the interviewer to refute your claim.

If you are coming to the interview unemployed, from a recently closed consulting practice or small business, or any other circumstance that makes it look like you are off the road to career success, here are the kinds of interviewer questions you can expect to face—and the kinds of answers you should be prepared to give.

QUESTIONS AND ANSWERS FOR THE UNEMPLOYED JOB SEEKER	
Question	**Answer**
Why did you leave your last job?	The company was recently bought by XYZ Corporation, and thirty accounting positions were consolidated into ten at their West Coast offices.
Why did you close your business or consulting practice?	After I spent years of successfully building my company, it was acquired by ABC Company. I am intrigued by the opportunity your vacancy represents.
Coming from your background, what appreciation could you possibly have for our career development expectations?	I am currently enrolled in the CFA study group and plan to take the Series I examination in June.

These kinds of reactions can build confidence in your interviewer—the stigma of failure is avoided. The employer wants to sense that you understand his or her needs, can meet them, and have the potential to fit in and grow. A traditional work history is not the only way for you to establish such a link with the employer—you might have to work harder at the logic of your presentation if you lack the step-by-step progression of readily understood and expected jobs, but it can be done.

Applying for a Less Prestigious Position

American business is going through an era in which management ranks are being thinned. For years layoffs affected mainly production workers, and the managers were spared. That is no longer the case, and you could find yourself out of work with no comparable positions available in the job market. When it happens, you apply for what you can get—and face the added interviewing burden of explaining why you are taking an apparent step *down* the career ladder.

RECOMMENDED APPROACH

When you approach the job interview as an "overqualified" candidate, you have several obstacles to surmount:

- You don't fit the usual experience pattern.
- You may pose a threat to the people who are hiring you.
- Your salary has been too high.
- You are accustomed to having more responsibility.

Here are some suggestions for dealing with the inevitable questions, whether they are posed directly or are hidden-agenda items that can be just as threatening to your candidacy.

CHALLENGES AND RESPONSES FOR CANDIDATES STEPPING DOWN TO LESSER JOBS	
Challenge	**Response**
You are used to dealing with bigger issues than you'll be facing here and will leave as soon as something more challenging comes along.	This is a permanent career realignment. My professional peers are experiencing the same thing I am. I want an opportunity to take one step back with the prospect of taking many steps forward as I prove myself here.
You won't be earning what you did at XYZ Corporation, and you'll be working just as hard. Will that be a morale problem for you?	I'm sure you'll compensate me fairly, and that's all I can ask. If I'm given the opportunity to show what I can be worth to your organization, the problem will eventually take care of itself.
What do I tell my own people who will view you as a threat?	Tell them you are in business to succeed and that you are hiring the best person for the job. I'm sure I'll have to perform to earn my promotions, not rely on the fact that I've already been to the next plateau.

JOB INTERVIEWING TIPS

When you enter the interview, unless it is apparent that your previous status is presenting no problem, take the initiative and speak to the obvious. Do it diplomatically—do not say "I know I probably pose a threat to you people, but...." Instead, gently, in the course of the interview, let it be known that you are aware of the possible sensitivities that naturally surround the selection of a person who is coming in from a more senior position. Choose your words and timing carefully, then make these points:

- You really do want the job in spite of the fact that it appears to be a step backward on your career ladder;

- You can live with a fair compensation package for the position being offered and recognize the potential differential with what you had been making;

- You expect to prove yourself just like everyone else, and you won't be coming in wearing vestiges of your former "rank" on your sleeve.

You need to portray yourself as a realistic candidate. While there is always the possibility that there is no sensitivity, and you certainly do not want to raise issues that are not troubling anyone, in most instances you would be safe to take a disarming approach to the situation and make the three points noted. It clears the air and, like affirmative action issues, ranks among the questions that interviewers are uncomfortable asking but may want to know. You can volunteer a well-thought-out story that puts you and your advanced status in both a positive and a nonthreatening light at the same time.

QUESTIONS AND ANSWERS FOR THE LESSER-POSITION CANDIDATE	
Question	**Answer**
Why would you want to come to work for us after working for the giant ABC Company?	Because there are things I do very well and I need a place in which to keep doing them. You are aware of the effect of mergers on people like us [. . . talking with a peer]. Frankly, I need to get started again, and this looks like a good place to grow in a new career.
Do you realize we do our own correspondence here on personal computers?	No, but what do you think of that resume? I did it on my PC at home. I've always consulted on the side and love formatting my own reports.
How do you feel about reporting to a person who would have been a subordinate in your last position?	I am applying for *this* position and fully expect to fit into *this* organization. No problem.

Student Work Experience

When you interview for your first professional position, you can help compensate for not having a working track record by making the most of your part-time experience. There is no better way to get the job you want after college than by having an established working relationship with the company as a highly regarded student-worker. Summer and part-time jobs lead to career positions for thousands of students every year. You can prepare for your interview in such a way as to take advantage of this kind of experience. Whether you are still a student accumulating your part-time experiences or a graduate seeking your first full-time job, the approach is much the same. This section distinguishes between the two and advises you on applying essentially the same logic to the two situations.

RECOMMENDED APPROACH

As a student interviewing for a part-time position with an organization, the best way to make yourself stand out is to show evidence of career thinking. You should be interested in the seasonal position for what it is, but aware of its implications for overall career development as well. If you are applying for your first full-time position, make the connection between your part-time experience and the job for which you are applying. You need to understand the linkage and communicate the value you place on the career-related part-time experience while interviewing in either situation.

This has to be done without overkill. You want to come across as someone aware of your present place in the order of things, but cognizant of its potential contribution to your career. You do that by expressing interest in both the position and the company—your awareness of what the firm does and its position in the marketplace, for example. Taking advantage of your research, you might mention a recent acquisition or new product as a way to show your awareness of the business world in general—and the interviewer's company in particular.

POINTS FOR STUDENTS AND RECENT GRADUATES TO MAKE	
Desired—Message	**Method of Relating It***
Part-time: I want this seasonal job—it is important to me for several reasons. *Full-time:* I valued my seasonal jobs—they were important to me for several reasons.	I value the work ethic and financial responsibility—this job will help me gain valuable work experience and avoid building debt as a student.

(cont'd)

POINTS FOR STUDENTS AND RECENT GRADUATES TO MAKE	
Desired—Message	**Method of Relating It***
Part-time: My education can contribute to doing this job well. *Full-time:* My education contributed a lot to doing my part-time jobs well, and you'll benefit as my employer from the experience I've already had in combining classroom and practical experience.	As a student of [engineering, marketing, or whatever] I have seen a lot of theory and case study examples of what you do at XYZ Corporation that would bring me to the job with a lot of orientation already in place anxious to apply it as a worker.
Part-time: I can see future possibilities with XYZ Corporation. *Full-time:* As a seasonal student worker I saw where my experience could make me a valuable full-time employee of XYZ Corporation.	I have a lot of respect for the market position of XYZ, have heard positive things about it as a place to build a career, and would welcome the opportunity for us to learn to know each other better in a worker-employer relationship.

*These are stated for the part-time applicant; rephrase them to show the value of *past* part-time experience to *future* full-time employment when interviewing for a career position.

JOB INTERVIEWING TIPS

As a student applying for a part-time position or a former student seeking a first career position, you do not have a track record of previous positions and responsibilities to explain to an interviewer. However, in either case you can use the interview to accomplish these objectives:

- Identify the part-time position you seek, and define the linkage with your studies and career aspirations—or make that connection retroactively if you are using the experience while interviewing for a career position;

- Qualify yourself for performing the required duties in either case—establish that you can do the job;

- Show career motivation as an applicant for part-time employment—or validate career interest as a prospective full-time employee by making the connection with past part-time positions.

Whether you are looking for seasonal or career employment, you need to show that you know what the job entails, can perform the necessary work, and that you see part-time employment, your studies, and your career as part of the same overall experience. This is what you want to communicate in the job interview:

> I am [...or was, in the case of a full-time applicant] a third-year electrical engineering student applying for the summer position as Field Engineering Aide III. My studies and prior Army experience qualify me for working in your testing environment, and I consider the seasonal position an exploratory one linked to what I hope will be a long professional affiliation with XYZ Corporation.

Your session might end with the interviewer inviting you to make a concluding comment on your own behalf. This is not the place to restate what has already been said, but it can be useful to focus on the objective and dispel any lingering problems. Here are examples of "problem" thinking that you may have sensed as your interview progressed—and appropriate points to offer in summary.

QUESTIONS AND ANSWERS FOR THE SEASONAL-JOB APPLICANT	
Question*	**Answer***
Why are you still a student at age twenty-eight?	Describe your military service as relevant to your career—possibly a year spent touring Europe after leaving the service and prior to returning to college.
Why would a person within a year of being a graduate engineer want a job like this?	Amplify your respect for learning the business from the inside out—this position could give you that perspective before crossing over to the professional level.
What kind of career expectations do you have?	If your awareness is sufficiently specific, briefly conclude with an expression of interest in exploring future employment with them in fiber optics transmission—or whatever.

*Each question and answer would be stated retrospectively in the case of a graduate making reference to past part-time experiences when interviewing for a full-time position.

Establishing Second Careers

Government and industry offer early retirement to reduce their work force in a non-destructive way. People leave completed careers still vigorous enough to want the continued ritual of the workplace—a reason for getting out of bed in the morning, socialization with coworkers, the satisfaction of accomplishing something, and—last, but not necessarily least—money. Whether you are a service member retired with a substantial pension in your forties, or an older clerical worker retired with a modest income by a large corporation, you could find yourself interviewing for a second career.

RECOMMENDED APPROACH

With one career behind you, your objective is to look ahead to the next job as an opportunity to use your past experiences and discover some satisfying new challenges. You are in transition and trying to make the case that you have something to offer the new employer. Here are some of the attitudes you want to anticipate encountering during your interview—and effective rebuttals for each:

ATTITUDES FACED BY AND RESPONSES OF SECOND-CAREER SEEKERS	
Attitude	**Response**
You are "retired." Why would I want to hire you?	In the modern workplace, careers are sometimes incremental—"retirement" is often a misnomer for a person successfully transitioning to another career stage.
Your background is from another environment entirely. How will you adapt to our situation?	Work is far more appropriately categorized by task than by employer. I have successfully managed people and resources for the past [number of] years, and I can do it for you.
What if you are looking to retire on the job?—my job!	The work ethic is very much a habit. My motivation in applying for this position is to continue deriving the satisfaction of a job well done. My references will vouch for my level of energy and commitment.

JOB INTERVIEWING TIPS

As a second-career person entering a job interview, you are interested in immediately establishing several basics:

- Identify the position or category of position you feel best qualified to handle as a second career;
- Establish your qualifications for the job;
- Express sincere motivation to pursue a second career and not leave your profession at your relatively young age.

While the points made during your job interview will vary by job and background, here is an example of how you might begin:

> I am a retired Navy senior enlisted woman with a successful paramedical career, and I'd like to become affiliated with a civilian health management organization. I'm a fully certified professional anxious to continue a rewarding health services career without interruption. I view my "retirement" as the end of a job, not the end of a career.

When you are given the opportunity during your interview, offer answers to some of the employer's questions that might otherwise have remained unsaid. Take these hidden-agenda doubts on directly rather than risk being hurt by negative conclusions that can come by default. Here are several examples and responses that can be helpful.

QUESTIONS AND ANSWERS FOR SECOND-CAREER CANDIDATES	
Question	**Answer**
How do I as an employer in the X business compare the certification of a specialist who has spent an entire career working in Y?	Professional certification for paraprofessionals in military health care facilities are the same as for those in civilian hospitals.

(cont'd)

Question	Answer
How will a person accustomed to having military rank and authority function in the less structured civilian environment?	Express your authority and rank functionally with examples of responsibility, rather than power and rank that will be more readily understood in the civilian sector.
You are in the service; how can I be assured you will be able to report for duty on the date you promise?	Mention that your retirement orders have been issued and that you will be separated from the service on a date comfortably in advance of your reporting date for the new position.

Looking for Flexibility

You might find yourself wanting to be employed in the regular work force, but with less than a full-time schedule and regular hours. You might be surprised to learn that the same requirement often exists on the hiring side of the equation—employers sometimes welcome the idea of having first-rate talent available to them on an "as needed" basis rather than full time. You start by communicating what you want and what you can deliver while working a nontraditional schedule. Approach the job interview by convincing the employer that you can deliver a lot of service while operating outside the office routine.

RECOMMENDED APPROACH

As a nontraditional worker in a job interview you need to represent yourself as a practicing professional whose only difference is situational. You are fully qualified but do not want to work full time. There are advantages to the employer as well as the worker in such arrangements, and you want to communicate them during your interview. Here are a few examples of traditional thinking that you might encounter with your interviewer, and suggested responses.

QUESTIONS FOR AND RESPONSES OF CANDIDATES SEEKING NONTRADITIONAL WORKING ARRANGEMENTS	
Question	**Response**
How could a part-time person possibly plan the annual meeting?	The job is a series of tasks to be accomplished, not hours to be logged. Let's discuss what has to be done, and I'll show you how I can do it.
How will you be able to get the "feel" of our organization if you are here only part time?	Involvement and perceptiveness are not measured by hours in the presence of others. Has my reading of your requirements so far been accurate?
How will we handle taxes and benefits?	There are several approaches. If you want me to be an employee, then pay the taxes and provide partial benefits. If you prefer, I'll work as an independent contractor, a more arm's-length relationship that can easily be arranged.

These are representative of the issues that might arise. If you have a particular orientation or want to steer the hiring in a certain direction, things such as the independent contractor versus part-time employee arrangement can be given greater emphasis during your interview. My book *The Home Business Bible* (John Wiley & Sons, 1994) covers these topics if you need further information.

JOB INTERVIEWING TIPS

You want to enter your interview as a serious, fully qualified candidate with the additional advantage of bringing flexibility to the employer. You might consider doing it this way:

I am a paralegal with six years' experience preparing corporate documents for law firms, and I'm looking for part-time employment in that specialty. I'd prefer to operate as an independent contractor and do the work in my home office. You don't have to be concerned about my professionalism and respect for confidentiality. The references I provided will be glad to establish those for you.

In this case you took advantage of the opportunity to introduce yourself at the start of the interview to describe your desired situation, the terms under which the work would be accomplished, and preempted an expected question about professionalism and confidentiality. You have laid the groundwork for responding to the interviewer's questions regarding your educational qualifications, specific abilities, and achievements. If you sense that it would be helpful, volunteer your reason for wanting the flexibility; since equal opportunity regulations keep interviewers from inquiring about family status, a comment like this might clear the air and help your cause.

> After six years of successful full-time employment in two law firms, I want to continue my professional pursuits privately for several years to give me the flexibility to raise my young children at home.

Another purely functional reason that has nothing to do with affirmative action could be:

> I'm building a consulting practice with clients that are not at all like yours. So I am in a position to use my talents on your behalf in the hours that I don't have committed and still not compete with you. I think we can help each other.

Coming from Other Countries and Cultures

The United States is still a melting pot for the special talents of people who join its work force with education and experience from other countries. The challenge for those job seekers is in translating their talents into terms that can be readily understood by U.S. employers. As a foreign worker, your job interview is an opportunity to simplify your situation for the employer—demystify the jumble of different-looking things in your resume and bring your real skills into focus.

RECOMMENDED APPROACH

You begin preparing for the interview by clarifying your own notion of where your experience fits in the American job market. If you need assistance, ask a friend who is familiar with jobs and qualifications in this country to help you translate your background into terms that will be recognized here. You should prepare thoroughly for the interview by doing the research necessary to understand what the company does and where it fits into its industry. Go the extra distance and match your experience to the company's operations—picture how your career would have unfolded in that corporate environment. It will put you in a better position to respond meaningfully during the interview.

JOB INTERVIEWING TIPS

If you are an engineer, you come to the interview with a common technical language that makes communicating with your interviewer easier. As a candidate with less-well-defined skills—a manager, perhaps—you have to make a greater effort to be sure your interviewer comprehends the connection between your background and his or her needs.

You approach the substance of the interview in much the same way as any other candidate—establishing your suitability for the job by describing your background, and making a case for what you have to offer. Where things get different for you as an applicant from another culture is establishing that certain peripheral things will not be a problem. Here are several examples of things you have to be prepared to address in the course of your interview.

INTERVIEWING CONCERNS AND POSSIBLE SOLUTIONS FOR THE FOREIGN CANDIDATE	
Concern	**Possible Solution**
My schooling was not in a system equivalent to American schools and colleges.	Sort your educational experiences into categories that equate to American levels—high school, junior college, trade school, or college. Employers may have to establish that you meet minimum requirements for the job and will need your assistance in making the case.
I will need my employer's support with visa considerations. How do I treat that subject?	Be honest about your immigration status, but do not make an issue of it. Objectively state the category that you hold and that to which you aspire. Leave the details of what that all means until you have an offer, if possible.

(cont'd)

Concern	Possible Solution
I want to establish that I can function in the American culture—language and customs.	Demonstrate what you have done— earned a degree attending an American college, held a job that clearly required English language proficiency, etc.

In the final analysis, the foreign student or worker faces the same problem as any other job candidate—making the point as directly and convincingly as possible that you know what the job entails and that you can do it. Your job interview is your best opportunity to make the case personally.

You will find a chapter that parallels this one and covers the same issues for the task of resume writing in my book *Resumes That Mean Business Third Edition* (Random House, 1999). If you approach a job search from the position of a nontraditional applicant, you will find that source particularly helpful in preparing your resume and cover letter.

SUMMARY CHECKLIST: SPECIAL SITUATIONS

- People in special situations benefit from using special approaches to their job interviews.

- A properly prepared nontraditional candidate can use his or her special circumstances to make the job interview more impressive than traditional career path competitors.

- Unemployment, mergers and reorganizations, self-employment, family obligations, and periods of full-time study can take you temporarily off the traditional career path and require special approaches for returning.

- You can anticipate and prepare yourself for the kinds of questions asked of candidates coming to an interview in these special situations.

PART

III

JOB SEARCH CORRESPONDENCE

11

WRITING THE LETTERS

The letters you send with your resume are among the most important communications you have with a hiring official. They are tangible representations of you that are shared with others as candidates are discussed and sorted. These letters play a significant role in determining your fate throughout the hiring cycle.

People who screen resumes look for reasons to set them aside. Their challenge is to reduce a stack of hundreds to the dozen that will receive careful scrutiny. Among the first criteria used to judge your packet are letter content and presentation. At various levels of consciousness, reviewers consider these factors:

- Is the letter written on clean, neat paper of a conventional business size, weight, and color?

- Is the letter written on only one side of the page?

- Am I reading a letter custom-written for this position or is it bulk mail?

- Does the letter correctly address a specific person involved in the hiring?

- Does the letter make it easy to find what I want to know about the applicant?

- Is the typing professional?

- Are the spelling and grammar correct?

- Is the letter phrased in a contemporary, unaffected style that sounds neither like a government regulation nor a letter from camp?

- Does the letter signal familiarity with the employer's organization and mission?

- Was the letter professionally produced on a business-grade printer—not on a low-resolution dot-matrix printer; not a mismatched, typed address inserted on a mass-produced letter?

- Does the letter use a conventional business typeface or something too scriptlike and highly stylized for the occasion?

- Has the letter been proofread and corrected professionally—no disconnects, obvious errors, or sloppy corrections?

- Is the letter personally signed?

Although an irresistibly attractive candidate might convey his or her credentials in a letter containing one or more of the problems mentioned above, don't count on being that person. In modern employee selection there are many applicants, and several of them usually are comparably attractive—so the quality of your correspondence matters.

Think of the entire stream of correspondence you will generate as you pursue leads, have interviews, field offers, and accept a position. Seat yourself on the final selection committee and picture the desirability of being represented by a matched set of coordinated, consistent correspondence. It speaks volumes about what can be expected as you complete work assignments on the job.

Put your resume and letters on the same kind of paper, use the same typeface, and remember that even your envelopes can find their way to the decision makers— avoid carelessly aligned dot matrix labels and scribbled addresses that you assume won't be seen by anyone beyond the mailroom. And don't forget to make your correspondence readable by the electronic scanning devices that process letters and resumes at a growing number of companies. Tips for electronic resumes are found in the author's *Resumes That Mean Business, Third Edition*.

Although you may not use them all, here is a series of job search letters to consider. Each letter has a place in securing your next position and—nearly as important—preparing for hiring cycles to follow in the years ahead. Fully developed examples of the letters follow these descriptive sketches:

- *Response to a Classified Ad: Comparison Points Letter*—This is the letter you write in response to an advertised position. In it you match what the employer asks for with your qualifications, point for point.

- *Response to a Specific Position Announcement: Conventional Letter*—This is the letter normally written in response to a position announcement.

- *Unsolicited Letter to an Executive Recruiter*—This letter announces your availability to an executive recruiter.

- *Availability Announcement Letter*—This letter makes your availability known broadly in your field.

- *Contact-Generating Letter*—This letter is used to refresh the memory of associates who are already in your network and ask them to suggest the names of others who might help.

- *Follow-up Letter*—This is the letter you send after a telephone or personal interview.

- *Bridge-Building Letter*—This letter is for leaving behind good feelings after a hiring cycle has not produced a job for you. The turndown might have come from you or the employer, but the objective is the same—leave everyone smiling and favorably disposed to hire you next time or, at least, to speak kindly of you.

- *Rejecting an Offer Letter*—This is a letter designed to say no to an offer but leave you in the employer's good graces.

- *Accepting an Offer Letter*—This letter is used to say yes to an offer and reaffirm the conditions of employment.

- *Resignation Letter*—This letter gives notice to your present employer, offers your assistance during the transition, and lets you part friends.

- *Thanks for Helping Letter*—This letter closes the loop with everyone who helped you this time, to ensure they'll be there next time.

You will benefit from reviewing the summary points following all of the letters, whether or not you use the particular letter. The advice usually generalizes to many kinds of correspondence, and it is not necessarily repeated for each sample letter.

RESPONSE TO A CLASSIFIED AD: COMPARISON POINTS LETTER

CAROL J. SEEKER
145 North Arlington Street, #903
Kingston, NY 12401
914-341-1001 Residence

May 24, 1999

John H. Wilson
Collections Manager
c/o Human Resources, Attn: DF/CA
TEC State Bank
7100 Takoma Drive
Falls Church, VA 22044

Dear Mr. Wilson:

Please consider this letter and the accompanying resume to be my application for the Home Equity Collector position you advertised in the Sunday, May 23, 1999, edition of *The Washington Post.*

My resume provides more details, but here is a quick comparison of your needs and my preparation to meet them.

• YOUR REQUIREMENT: Independent, detail-oriented worker with excellent verbal and written communication skills in financial collections.

• MY PREPARATION: Prepared collection cases, crafted mail solicitations, and conducted follow-up calls for overdue credit card customers at the National Credit Union for the past three years.

• YOUR REQUIREMENT: Lotus 1-2-3 and word processing experience.

• MY PREPARATION: Used Lotus 1-2-3 and WordPerfect in case load management and direct mail solicitations.

• YOUR REQUIREMENT: Knowledge of bankruptcy, foreclosure, and collection laws and practices.

• MY PREPARATION: In addition to my bachelor's degree in marketing management, I have taken evening courses in real estate law and finance.

Thank you for your consideration, and I look forward to hearing from you. I would welcome the opportunity to provide additional information and to meet with you personally at your earliest convenience.

Sincerely,

Carol J. Seeker

attachment

Comments on Carol's Letter:

- This letter is written in response to a newspaper advertisement. It is easily modified to accommodate a different source announcing a different position.

- She correctly identified the position in her letter.

- She determined the name of the hiring official but respected the protocol of sending her letter in care of the human resources department cited in the ad. This is a judgment call; contact the manager directly if you have reason to believe your resume will not get past human resources. In this case, her qualifications are a good match to the position, and she should be considered. Another option is to send an information copy to the hiring official. Ideally, you want to avoid alienating human resources by going around them, but your objective is to have your application seen by the decision maker. If you can't determine internal company relationships, make follow-up calls to ensure your application made it beyond personnel.

- This letter abandons the popular practice of side-by-side columns in "your requirements/my qualifications"–style letters because electronic scanners digest single-column correspondence better than multiple columns.

- It is not necessary to give details such as college name since a resume accompanies the letter.

- If you prefer not to be contacted at work, add a sentence that says so and suggests the way to reach you.

- If you will be traveling, mention the dates and suggest a way to reach you.

RESPONSE TO A SPECIFIC POSITION ANNOUNCEMENT: CONVENTIONAL LETTER

CARL T. APPLICANT
145 South Response Street, #411
Kingston, NY 12401
914-341-1001

April 5, 1999

Kristina R. Bentrex
Project Manager (SYS/WF)
WinSystems Corporation
8931 Pinecrest Road
Atlanta, GA 30305

Dear Ms. Bentrex:

I am responding to your position announcement #2709-SYS/WF, dated April 4, 1999, for Systems Engineers. The opportunity was brought to my attention by Charles Planner, a project engineer at your firm. Mr. Planner and I collaborated on a contract at Research Signal several years ago.

As the accompanying resume details, I have the background you seek. In brief:

• I hold a bachelor's degree in electrical engineering from the University of Maryland.

• I have held a variety of positions in ISDN and Digital Signal Processing in worldwide telecommunications environments.

• My duties over the past ten years included project support, design analysis, specification identification, hardware and software allocation, and customized system design.

• I have performed these functions with a diverse product line that included both voice and data communications.

• My experience includes HOL, C, and Assembly (Intel 186/486) languages and a thorough familiarity with ISDN protocols.

I am familiar with your company's international reputation and market position since I have worked for your competitors in these markets. I genuinely respect and admire WinSystems Corporation, and I would welcome the opportunity to discuss the systems engineering position with you at your earliest convenience. In the interim, please feel free to discuss my background with Mr. Planner or anyone else in our industry.

Sincerely yours,

Carl T. Applicant

enclosure

Comments on Carl's Letter:

- He knows the name and title of the hiring official and communicates with her directly since he has inside information that this would be a welcome approach.

- He identifies by name and position a former colleague he knows would comment favorably about him if asked.

- He uses the language of the business to succinctly and authoritatively establish that he has the desired credentials.

- Going beyond the mention of an acquaintance in the company, he telegraphs that he knows the company culture and would function comfortably in it.

- He asks for the interview—like the salesperson who always asks for the sale.

UNSOLICITED LETTER TO AN EXECUTIVE RECRUITER

JOHN T. HARDER
145 South Response Street, #411
Kingston, NY 12401
914-341-1001 Office
914-341-2111 Residence

June 22, 1999

Robert G. Cumberland
Coldwell, Sampson and Associates
8931 Pinecrest Road, Suite 202
Lake Buena Vista, FL 32830

Dear Mr. Cumberland:

I am sending my resume with a request that you keep me in mind as you work with companies that may be looking for a business development manager in environmental services. My position for the past three years as director of sales for ABF Corporation prepares me well for a similar position in a larger organization.

The following things should interest a prospective employer:

· Successful penetration of new urban markets in the highly competitive mid-Atlantic Region—I have increased new client contracts by an average of 18 percent annually since joining the firm.

· Secured invitations to present marketing briefing on company services to growth sector companies—I am especially effective in reaching the institutional health care group, where contracts have grown by 15 percent during my tenure.

· Experienced in generating technical proposals and contracts, where my efforts have reduced closing expenses 8 percent by eliminating separate staffing.

· Particularly successful in telling the company's story in the public relations arena.

The resume that accompanies this letter spells out my precise work experience and educational preparation. My wife and I are particularly fond of the Southeast but would relocate anywhere except the New York metropol-itan area for the right opportunity. I am currently earning $55,000 annu-ally with benefits, and I expect approximately a 20 percent increase in salary and comparable benefits to justify a move, although I could be more flexible in a situation offering exceptional future growth potential.

Please call if you feel my credentials would be of interest to a client. You can reach me at home, or a discreet call to the office is fine. Please treat this contact confidentially and clear each release of my credentials with me. I look forward to hearing from you, and I will contact your office soon to determine the status of my inquiry.

Sincerely,

John T. Harder

attachment

Comments on John's Letter:

- A specific recruiter with an interest in his specialty was selected from a published guide or at the suggestion of someone in the industry.

- He immediately establishes that he is in the recruiter's area of interest, has been on the job a respectable period of years (he is not "job hopping"), and is a viable candidate seeking to make a logical progression in his field.

- He provides the recruiter with specific accomplishments that demon-strate his marketability.

- He identifies his salary and experience ranges, sets realistic growth ex-pectations, and shows flexibility.

- He defines his geographic preferences and limitations and verifies that both he and his spouse are prepared to relocate—the latter is something a recruiter may be reluctant to ask but wants to know before expending effort that may come to nothing if the spouse vetoes the move.

- He okays telephone contact at the office, requests confidentiality, and asks that his resume not be broadcast without his permission.

AVAILABILITY ANNOUNCEMENT
LETTER

W. EDITH DECKER, PH.D.
32 Lamp Post Lane
Towson, MD 21286
410-341-1001 Office
410-341-2111 Residence

July 13, 1999

Connie H. Packard
Government Consultants, Inc.
86 Beltway Plaza, Suite 500
Arlington, VA 22202

Dear Ms. Packard:

I am writing to make you aware of my plans to pursue a professional growth opportunity in the coming months when my present project is completed. As a successful consultant supporting federal contractors fulfilling re-engineering, work group facilitation, and change management obligations, I knew our interests would be compatible.

As you can determine more precisely from the accompanying resume, I have:

• An earned doctorate in management from the University of Chicago

• Eight years of successful experience with three regional consulting firms specializing in short-duration service contracts with federal agencies having international operations

• A demonstrated willingness to work for extended periods of temporary duty overseas

• Performance assessment and technology standards experience

- CSI clearances

- Strong communication skills

My salary requirements are in the $60,000 range.

Hopefully these introductory comments will help you judge my potential, and I am confident that a meeting in which we can elaborate on these points would be beneficial. Thank you for your interest. I will call next week to see when we can get together.

Sincerely,

W. Edith Decker, Ph.D.

P.S. Please share my credentials with associates who might be interested.

attachment

Comments on Edith's Letter:

- The prominent display of an academic credential is not always desirable; in this case, however, it instantly satisfies a prominent criterion for the consulting position she seeks and is acceptable.

- She explains that this is a general notice of future availability and that she is presently employed in the kind of work she seeks.

- She presents the highlights of her credentials in a format easily digested and remembered by someone who will file her letter for future reference.

- She addresses potential reservations, such as willingness to travel.

- Valuable clearances are noted.

- She encourages future contact and takes the initiative in setting up an appointment.

- She asks that her availability be made known to others.

- She states her salary requirements to avoid unrealistic inquiries.

CONTACT-GENERATING LETTER

BLAKE K. NACKENOUR
5 Smith Street, #104
Prince Frederick, MD 20678
410-341-2111 Residence

July 15, 1999

Robert G. Sampson
Coldwell, Sampson and Associates
8931 Pinecrest Road, Suite 202
Lake Buena Vista, FL 32830

Dear Mr. Sampson:

I am writing to enlist your help in my job search. No, I am not asking you for a job, but I would appreciate it if you would review my resume, retain it for future reference, and share it with others who might be interested in someone with my background.

I was caught in the downsizing of XYZ Corporation's headquarters in nearby Baltimore, MD, last spring, about which you may be aware. Although I remain optimistic about the future, the job market for our career field is quite competitive at the present time. That is why I am taking the extraordinary step of contacting associates like you and requesting the same kind of assistance I would provide if our situations were reversed.

Although I have done my best to identify people who are influential in the business, your help in providing several more useful contacts would be most appreciated. I will call you in about a week to get their names and listen to any other advice you might like to offer.

In the briefest of summaries, here is what you will find explained more fully in the accompanying resume about my qualifications:

- Southeast Regional Field Training Manager, XYZ Corporation, 5 years
- Managed the growth and development of customer training
- Proven expertise in instruction and course design and development
- Highly proficient in the use of technologically advanced training media
- Innovative use of CBT, multimedia, self-paced, and online training tools

Thank you for your willingness to assist me in re-entering the profession. I look forward to speaking with you next week. If you prefer to contact me sooner, you can reach me at the residence number listed above or through Smithson Outplacement Services, 410-444-0001, extension 307.

Sincerely yours,

Blake K. Nackenour

enclosure

Comments on Blake's Letter:

- Contact-generating, sometimes referred to as networking, letters often go to people you know well. Be as familiar and personal as the relationship allows, but when in doubt, keep the tone professional.

- A combination of candor about needing help and optimism about the future is an effective element in a contact-generating letter.

- He helps the other person experience the "there but for the grace of God go I" sentiment by drawing comparisons and mentioning his willingness to help if the tables were turned.

- He summarizes his qualifications.

- He asks for help like a salesperson asking for the sale. He promises follow-through and encourages the person to contact him.

FOLLOW-UP LETTER

WALDO J. STRIPE
145 Prospect Street
Waltham, MA 02154
781-341-1001 Office
781-341-2111 Residence

September 29, 1999

Phyllis M. Xenia
Manager, Imaging Sciences Division
The Malcolm Deen Companies
8931 Dolphin Road, Suite 202
Coral Springs, FL 33065

Dear Ms. Xenia:

I am writing to thank you for the September 28th interview for the Image Scientist, Lead Engineer position at your Orlando plant. It was especially useful to meet you there and tour the new facilities. I was genuinely impressed with the color printer technology processes you have concentrated at this location.

As lead engineer on the focus team, I would look forward to the challenge of directing Deen's efforts in building optical measurement systems for image and color analysis. I came away from the visit and our stimulating conversations with ideas I look forward to sharing the next time we meet. Specifically, I would like to get your reaction to my thinking regarding the problems your staff discussed in the areas of vision systems hardware design and image processing software. I am confident you will find my comments useful in the crucial area of color reproduction evaluation methods.

You evaluate many people in the course of hiring, so let me recap my qualifications:

- MS in Engineering/Image Science
- 4 years of imaging and color analysis experience with DEF

- Specializations in visual measurements and psychophysics
- Knowledge of home and business computers and printers
- High-level programming abilities
- Excellent management and communication skills

I was impressed with the facilities, the scientific and commercial challenges facing the lead engineer, and your vision for the position. If you end the search sharing my judgment that I am the person for the job, I am certain we can come to terms on a compensation package that would offer the growth I seek.

If I can further substantiate my ability to meet your needs at Orlando, please call me at home or work. My e-mail address is: StripeW@def.iss.com, if that would be more convenient. Thanks again for your time. I look forward to hearing from you.

Sincerely yours,

Waldo J. Stripe

Comments on Waldo's Letter:

- Waldo was careful to get his interviewer's name and title correct, even if he had to call and verify it.

- He mentions specifics that demonstrate his grasp of her requirements.

- He specifically says how he relates to the challenges ahead and offers to share his insights at their next interview—as he increases its likelihood by suggesting what amounts to a free consultation on her problems.

- Waldo is realistic about not being the only candidate, and he restates his strengths.

- He explicitly welcomes the challenge and punctuates the thought by adding commercial sensitivity to the expected scientific one.

- He judges himself to be the person for the job but acknowledges that the choice is hers.

- He suggests that they can reach agreeable terms and invites further contact.

BRIDGE-BUILDING LETTER

GERALDINE P. HAYES
973 Stemm Creek Parkway
Palo Alto, CA 94304
650-341-2111 Residence
hayesg@jobwk.cko.com

January 22, 1999

Kirk B. Wonderly
Timberlane, Booth & Chairwood
9455-67 Manufacturers' Road, NE
Fairfield, OH 45014

Dear Mr. Wonderly:

Although I was disappointed not to receive the merchandising management position for which I was considered, I want to thank you for the interview and wish you success with the person you hired. In today's fluid job market, we could well meet again, and I want you to keep me in mind the next time you or others you know in the industry are looking for management talent.

I value professional relationships developed in meetings like we had exploring this vacancy. I learned things from you, acquired respect for your way of doing business, and would welcome the opportunity to work with you in the future, possibly in another capacity. I hope that you feel the same and would be comfortable calling on me whenever such contact might be advantageous to either of us.

Thanks again for the courtesies extended during the selection process. I look forward to hearing from you in the future.

Sincerely,

Geraldine P. Hayes

Comments on Geraldine's Letter:

- Her e-mail address is provided as part of the letterhead. Whether or not it is used by the recipient, it communicates familiarity with current technology.

- For the cost of a stamp and the time to write a final letter, she remains a player in the mind of someone with the power to hire.

- Her realistic observations about the job market and her place in it should register favorably with the recipient.

- The compliments are professional and not overdone, and everyone likes to hear them.

- She presumes a continuing professional relationship and invites future contact.

REJECTING AN OFFER LETTER

CLYDE I. PACKARD
145 South Response Street,   411
Kansas City, MO 64106
816-341-1001 Office
816-341-2111 Residence

February 2, 1999

Samuel C. Rockbridge, Jr.
Vice President, Human Resources
Stovemaster Manufacturing Company
Jackson, MS 39201

Dear Mr. Rockbridge:

I spent last evening giving thorough consideration to your offer of a position as Safety Manager with Stovemaster Manufacturing. Although there are many attractive aspects to the opportunity, I came to the conclusion that it would not be the right move for me in my circumstances.

You may recall commenting Monday that one purpose of the interview process is to give both the candidate and the company the opportunity to make the right decision. I am grateful for that advice and for your candor in describing my prospects for growth in the position.

When I evaluated everything objectively, I concluded that I had not satisfied my own criteria for selecting my next position. You have an impressive organization, and if I were at an earlier stage of my professional growth I would relish a place on your team.

Thank you for the offer; but I must decline. All the best in your future endeavors. Please let me know if I can ever be of assistance to you or Stovemaster Manufacturing.

Sincerely,

Clyde I. Packard

Comments on Clyde's Letter:

- Although it may not matter in a rejection letter, note that his choice of a script typeface is attractive but difficult for the scanner of a computerized applicant tracking system to read.

- Clyde indicates that his decision was made after careful thought—he had been a serious candidate, not someone wasting the company's time.

- Insufficient prospect for growth is always an acceptable reason for saying no.

- Referring to the hiring official's comment that helped him reach the right decision makes the conclusion mutually acceptable.

- Saying he would have welcomed a place on the team at the right point in his career minimizes thoughts of broader negatives—the turndown was for specific and limited reasons.

ACCEPTING AN OFFER LETTER

HELEN B. JENSEN
Redoubt Street, South, #881
Atlanta, GA 30346
404-341-1001 Office
404-341-2111 Residence

March 2, 1999

Michael N. Arrowsmith
Senior Vice President, Marketing
The ABC Companies, Ltd.
Eden Prairie, MN 55334

Dear Mr. Arrowsmith:

I want to confirm our telephone conversation of yesterday afternoon in which you offered me the position of District Sales Manager with The ABC Companies, Ltd. The terms of employment described in the fax that followed are consistent with our negotiations, and I look forward to completing and returning the formal contract when I receive it in several days.

As was evident during the interviews, we share a mutual enthusiasm about the prospects of leading the company to new highs in sales and market penetration. I can't wait to begin.

Please extend my appreciation to your colleagues who informed me so thoroughly about the challenges and opportunities associated with the position. I look forward to confirming their confidence in me.

Let me know if there is anything I can do to get a head start or otherwise facilitate the transition.

Yours truly,

Helen B. Jensen

Comments on Helen's Letter:

- While being pleasant and properly enthusiastic about accepting the position, Helen confirms the conditions of employment and asks for the formal contract.

- She cites points of agreement and says she is ready to begin.

- Her letter extends to kind words about others in the company on whom her success will depend.

- Concluding her acceptance with a commitment to start assuming responsibilities now makes her sound like a desirable employee.

RESIGNATION LETTER

NORWOOD D. BLACK
145 South Response Street, #993
Kingston, NY 12401
914-341-1001 Office
914-341-2111 Residence

February 7, 1999

Nadine V. Upland
Senior Scientist
Coldwell, Sampson and Associates
8931 Pinecrest Road, Suite 202
Kingston, NY 12401

Dear Ms. Upland:

Please accept this letter as my resignation from my position at Coldwell, Sampson and Associates. I begin new duties as senior scientist with the Benning Group in Green Spring, SC, on March 1, 1999. While some flexibility is possible, I intend to make February 21 my last day with the company unless a slightly different schedule is desirable from your perspective.

I'm sure you're aware of my favorable feelings about my Coldwell, Sampson experience. You and my other colleagues have been a pleasure to work with, both professionally and personally. The significant step forward that I am about to take is largely a result of my work here. I value your contributions to my development, and I will always be grateful.

If there is anything I can do, now or after I leave, to make things easier for my sucessor, just let me know. I look forward to our continued professional association in the years ahead, and I wish you and the Coldwell, Sampson family the best.

Yours truly,

Norwood D. Black

Comments on Norwood's Letter:

- Resignation letters generally follow a conversation in which the intention to resign is conveyed personally.

- He states for the record when he will leave, while extending whatever flexibility is possible.

- Two weeks is the minimum notice in most situations, but staying too long after announcing your departure is also unwise. The best advice is to leave promptly and offer to assist your successor or those who will assume your responsibilities.

- Resignation letters are for accentuating the positive, eliminating the negative. Few working relationships are perfect, but the focus should be on the future and a positive view of the past. Set the stage for future pleasantries as your professional paths cross.

THANKS FOR HELPING LETTER

FRANKLIN P. WARNER, JR.
45 South Depot Street, #11
Kingston, NY 12401
914-341-1201 Office
914-341-3111 Residence

April 2, 1999

Roberta L. Calvert
Sampson and Associates
89 Crest Road, Suite 207
Amherst, NY 14228

Dear Ms. Calvert:

I wanted to let you know that I successfully concluded my job search and began my new position as an account executive with the Wilson Group last week. The job is just what I had been looking for, and it should provide the perfect outlet for the creative energies you so graciously recognized in me when we discussed my plans a few weeks ago.

The letters of recommendation you provided and telephone reference checks you accommodated were greatly appreciated. I have come to understand the value of professional friendships like yours and the important role they play in securing occupational advancement.

Thanks again for helping. If there is anything I can do for you in the future, please don't hesitate to ask.

Sincerely,

Franklin P. Warner, Jr.

Comments on Franklin's Letter:

- This is a letter to a reference. It could as easily have been written to anyone who assisted in the job search.

- Franklin personalized the note of thanks by relating a specific that the recipient would recall.

- He thanks the person for specific things he knows she did for him—letters and telephone calls.

- He offers to repay the favor.

Suggestions on Style

Although you might find the occasion to use nearly any style in your job search correspondence, the examples that follow are things you probably want to avoid.

1. Being presumptuous:

- Would you like to find the ideal person to fill your position? If you are, well here I am...

- It was clear to me that you were impressed by my...

- One of your clients needs me and...

- Eleven reasons to hire John Smith:

2. Passive voice:

- AWKWARD: Having spent many years...

  BETTER: I have spent many years...

- AWKWARD: Hoping to meet you personally when...

  BETTER: I hope to meet you when...

- AWKWARD: I was surprised to have been contacted by...

  BETTER: I was surprised when I was contacted by...

3. Making statements unnecessarily complicated:

- AWKWARD: With this letter and resume I would like to...

  BETTER: This letter and resume...

- AWKWARD: As you can see from the enclosed resume...

  BETTER: My resume shows...

- AWKWARD: Please feel free to share my credentials with any of your associates who you feel might be interested.

  BETTER: Please share my credentials with interested associates.

- AWKWARD: It is not that I would absolutely never...

  BETTER: I would not...

- AWKWARD: It is my sincere hope that this resume describes my qualifications for...

  BETTER: This resume describes my qualifications for...

- AWKWARD: I fervently wish I had the opportunity to express to you personally...

  BETTER: I wish I could tell you...

- AWKWARD: As per our conversation of...

  BETTER: When we spoke on...

- AWKWARD: I would like to take this opportunity to thank you so very much for...

  BETTER: Thank you for...

- AWKWARD: It was indeed my great pleasure to have joined you for...

  BETTER: I enjoyed joining you for...

- AWKWARD: As of this date it is my intention to...

  BETTER: Today I...

- AWKWARD: We in the software development community...

  BETTER: Software developers...

4. Clichés:

- I thrive on challenges, lead by my own example, am eternally optimistic, and will remain loyal to your organization through thick and thin.

- I represent the brightest and the best...

- I am a self-starter who...

- Gone but not forgotten, you surely recall speaking with me last month about...

5. Unprofessional:

- Let me be brief. I want a job with your company. Read my resume and call me! [This was the applicant's entire cover letter.]

- Hi John: Just thought I'd take a few minutes and...

- You are the best-looking woman I've ever had an interview with and...

- I'll give you a buzz next week regarding...

Strive for attention-getting introductory statements that are based on demonstrated familiarity with the job, company, current market conditions, a relevant bit of news, awareness of new technology, or the mention of someone whose familiarity with your work would be valued. For the balance of the letter, phrase your thoughts the way you would say the same things in polite, not overly formal or informal, conversation. The test: Say it out loud, and if it doesn't sound like you speaking, simplify the sentence and be pleasantly direct.

BIBLIOGRAPHY

Allen, Jeffrey G. *Jeff Allen's Best: Get the Interview.* New York: John Wiley & Sons, 1990.
———. *Jeff Allen's Best: Win the Job.* New York: John Wiley & Sons, 1990.
Application of the Employee Polygraph Protection Act of 1988; Final Rule. *Federal Register*, March 4, 1991.
Artise, John. "Find the Hidden Agenda in Interview Questions." *The Best of the National Business Employment Weekly.* New York: Dow Jones (undated).
Bacas, Harry. "Hiring the Best." *Nation's Business*, October 1987, pp. 68–71.
Barrett, Laurence I. "Cheating on the Tests." *Time*, June 3, 1991, p. 57.
Beardsley, Tim. "Mind Reader: Do Personality Tests Pick Out Bad Apples?" *Scientific American*, April 1991, pp. 154–56.
Bernstein, Amy. "Rent-an-image." *U.S. News & World Report*, April 1, 1991, p. 14.
Biegeleisen, J. I. *Make Your Job Interview a Success*, 3rd ed. New York: Prentice Hall Press/Simon & Schuster, 1991.
Bolles, Richard N. *What Color Is Your Parachute?* Berkeley, Calif.: Ten Speed Press, 1998.
Braham, James. "Hiring Mr. Wrong." *Industry Week*, March 7, 1988, pp. 31–34.
Brown, Paul B. "Every Picture Tells a Story." *INC.*, August 1987, pp. 18–21.
Brown, Thomas L. "The Mommy Track: Is It Legal?" *Industry Week*, October 2, 1989, p. 24.
Byrne, John. "All the Right Moves for Interviewers." *Business Week*, September 17, 1990, p. 156.
Caminiti, Susan. "Watch Out, John Hancock." *Fortune*, January 4, 1988, p. 82.
Carey, James. "Go with the Flow." *Harper's Magazine*, July 1990, p. 23.
Charges: Filing a Charge. Washington, D.C.: U.S. Equal Employment Opportunity Commission, November 1988.
The Charging Party: Your Rights and Responsibilities. Washington, D.C.: U.S. Equal Employment Opportunity Commission, February 1990.
"Check It Out." *INC.*, November 1988, p. 148.
Copeland, Jeff B., et al. "The Revenge of the Fired." *Newsweek*, February 16, 1987, pp. 46–47.
Dumaine, Brian. "The New Art of Hiring Smart." *Fortune*, August 17, 1987, pp. 78–81.

Elder, Robert W., and Gerald R. Ferris, eds. *The Employment Interview: Theory, Research, and Practice.* Newbury Park, Calif.: Sage Publications, 1989.

Elsberry, Richard B. "Fired at 53." *The Best of the National Business Employment Weekly.* New York: Dow Jones (undated).

Eyler, David R. *The Executive Moonlighter: Building Your Next Career Without Leaving Your Present Job.* New York: John Wiley & Sons, 1989.

———. *Resumes That Mean Business, Third Edition.* New York: Random House, 1999.

———. *The Home Business Bible.* New York: John Wiley & Sons, 1994.

———, and Andrea P. Baridon. *More Than Friends, Less Than Lovers: Managing Sexual Attraction in the Workplace.* Los Angeles: Jeremy P. Tarcher, 1991.

Falvey, Jack. "Age 52 and Counting." *The Best of the National Business Employment Weekly.* New York: Dow Jones (undated).

———. "Congratulations, You're Fired." *The Best of the National Business Employment Weekly.* New York: Dow Jones (undated).

———. "Reentering the Work Force." *The Best of the National Business Employment Weekly.* New York: Dow Jones (undated).

"Foolish Interviews." *USAir Magazine,* April 1991, p. 11.

"Get the Bad News, Too." *INC.,* January 1989, p. 107.

Gibbs, Nancy. "Office Crimes." *Time,* October 21, 1991, pp. 52–64.

Gorman, Christine. "Honestly, Can We Trust You?" *Time,* January 23, 1989, p. 44.

Hafner, Katie, and Susan Garland. "Testing for Drug Use: Handle with Care." *Business Week,* March 28, 1988, p. 65.

Hayes, George W. "The Likability Quotient." *The Best of the National Business Employment Weekly.* New York: Dow Jones (undated).

"Hiring: An Eye for Detail," "Hands On: A Manager's Notebook," *INC.,* December 1988, p. 138.

Hoerr, John. "It's Getting Harder to Pass Out Pink Slips." *Business Week,* March 28, 1988, p. 68.

———, et al. "Privacy." *Business Week,* March 28, 1988, pp. 61–68.

Holland, John L. *The Psychology of Vocational Choice.* Waltham, Mass.: Blaisdell Publishing Company, 1966.

Jenks, James M. "Tactful Answers to Illegal Interview Questions." *The Best of the National Business Employment Weekly.* New York: Dow Jones (undated).

———, and Brian L. P. Zevnik. "ABC's of Job Interviewing." *Harvard Business Review,* July–August 1989, pp. 38–42.

"Julia Roberts: 20 Questions." *Playboy,* November 1991, pp. 151–57.

Manley, Marisa. "Employment Lines." *INC.,* June 1988, pp. 132–36.

———. "Information, Please." *INC.,* June 1989, pp. 135–39.

Mannix, Margaret, Diane Duke, and Marc Silver. "What References?" *U.S. News & World Report,* April 15, 1991, p. 74.

Moreau, Dan. "Answers That Get You Hired." *Changing Times,* April 1989, pp. 53–55.

Moskal, Brian S. "Can You Pass Muster?: How the Japanese Hire at Diamond-Star." *Industry Week,* February 15, 1988, p. 20.

Nine Forces Reshaping America. Alexandria, Va.: United Way/World Future Society, 1989.

NOTICE: Employee Polygraph Protection Act (WH Publication 1462). Washington, D.C.: U.S. Department of Labor, September 1988.

Ormont, Rhonda. "Let Me Introduce Myself." *The Best of the National Business Employment Weekly.* New York: Dow Jones (undated).

Part 1607—Uniform Guidelines on Employee Selection Procedures (1978). 29 CFR Chap. XIV (July 1, 1990 edition). Washington, D.C.: U.S. Equal Employment Opportunity Commission, July 1990.

Pave, Irene. "Job References: Handle with Care." *Business Week,* March 9, 1987, p. 124.

Perkoski, Robert R., and Kevin Collin. "Six Ways to Rescue a Bad Interview." *The Best of the National Business Employment Weekly.* New York: Dow Jones (undated).

Plawin, Paul. "Job Hunting Blunders You Don't Have to Make." *Changing Times,* December 1988, pp. 67–70.

Pooley, Eric, ed. "Act Like a Lawyer." *New York,* October 19, 1987, p. 40.

Posner, Bruce G. "Hiring the Best." *INC.,* April 1989, pp. 169–70.

Psychological Assessment Resources. *1991 Fall Catalog: Professional Testing Resources.* Odessa, Fla.: Psychological Assessment Resources, 1991.

Rachlin, Jill. "Big Signature, Little Person?" *U.S. News & World Report,* March 21, 1988, p. 69.

Richardson, Douglas B. "Battling Age Discrimination." *The Best of the National Business Employment Weekly.* New York: Dow Jones (undated).

———. "The Formula for Interview Success." *The Best of the National Business Employment Weekly.* New York: Dow Jones (undated).

Rohan, Thomas M. "New Tips on Screening Employees." *Industry Week,* January 4, 1988, pp. 33–35.

Satterfield, Mark. "Now, Do You Have Any Questions?" *The Best of the National Business Employment Weekly.* New York: Dow Jones (undated).

———. "Why Candidates Fail the Interview." *The Best of the National Business Employment Weekly.* New York: Dow Jones (undated).

———. "Why You Weren't Hired." *The Best of the National Business Employment Weekly.* New York: Dow Jones (undated).

Schabacker, Kirsten. "Candid Candidates: New and Revealing Interview Tactics." *Working Woman,* September 1990, pp. 62–63.

Seligman, Daniel. "Bias in the Casino." *Fortune,* April 10, 1989, pp. 153–54.

———. "More Normal Nonsense." *Fortune,* July 17, 1989, p. 118.

Serlen, Bruce. "Job Hunting at Forty Plus." *The Best of the National Business Employment Weekly.* New York: Dow Jones (undated).

Siegel, Eleanor. "Educational Needs Beyond the Classroom." *Publishers Weekly,* March 15, 1991, pp. 15–22.

Statement on pre-employment tests (untitled two-page handout). Washington, D.C.: U. S. Equal Employment Opportunity Commission (undated).

Stybel, Laurence J., and Maryanne Peabody. "Job Search Techniques for Shy Candidates." *The Best of the National Business Employment Weekly.* New York: Dow Jones (undated).

"This Is Your Life." *Harper's Magazine,* December 1989, pp. 19–22.

"A Tissue of Lies." *Fortune,* November 9, 1987, p. 12.

Tooley, Jo Ann. "Scaring Bosses into Silence." *U.S. News & World Report,* October 16, 1989, p. 125.

"Unemployment Strategies." *Harper's Magazine,* December 1989, p. 20.

User's Companion to Poor's Register: A Primer of 89 Proven Methods for Effectively Using Stan-

dard & Poor's Register of Corporations, Directors and Executives. New York: Standard & Poor's Corporation, 1983.

Welter, Therese R. "Interviewing for a Job——by Satellite." *Industry Week,* May 18, 1987, p. 94.

Wiener, Daniel P., et al. "A Road Map to That First Job." *U.S. News & World Report,* May 13, 1991, pp. 88–90.

INDEX

Now you're ready for your job interview. But is your resume?

Look for *Resumes That Mean Business, 3rd Edition!*

This book tells you how today's employers evaluate a resume and helps you create the right resume to land the job you want.

Includes **80 model resumes**–plus before-and-after examples of resume first aid. Simple resume templates clearly illustrate how to highlight your strengths while carefully addressing weak spots.

Fully updated for today's electronic workplace, including up-to-date information on:

- Using the Internet and other technology
- Creating an electronic resume
- Resumes for special situations: returning to the workplace, establishing a second career, and more

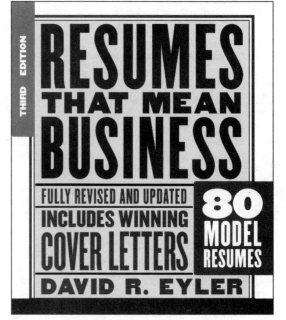

Show your prospective employer you mean business–every step of the way–with *Resumes That Mean Business*!

0-375-70469-8 $12.95 paperback

Available at bookstores everywhere or call 1-800-733-3000 to order.